AF394311

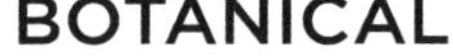

BOTANICAL

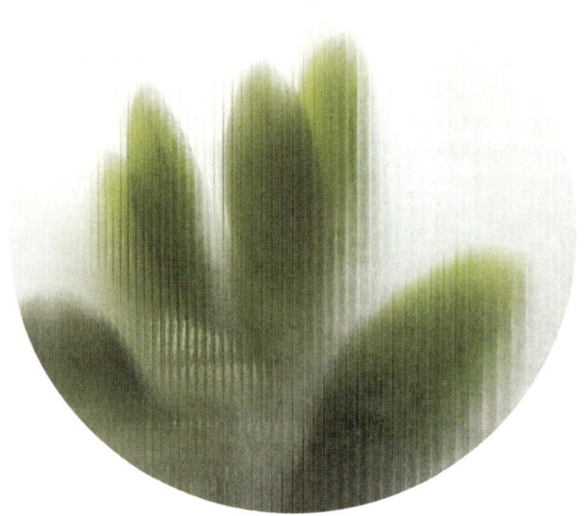

BOTANICAL

SAMUEL ZELLER

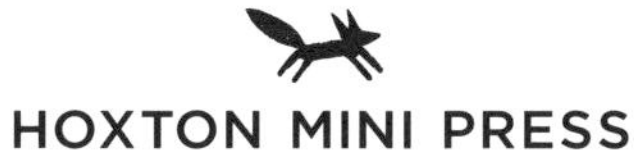

HOXTON MINI PRESS

From the series

TALES FROM THE CITY

Book Six

INTRODUCTION

by Rachel Segal Hamilton

Writing in 1914, the German poet Paul Scheerbart fantasised about doing away with bricks as a material for building and replacing them with 'lustrous, colourful, mystical and noble glass walls' to create nothing less than 'a paradise on Earth'. His words spring to mind when looking at Samuel Zeller's *Botanical* series. Gazing through the glass walls of greenhouses at plants encased inside like precious jewels is a magical experience. With their interplay of delicate light, rough texture and lush colour, his shots offer a spellbinding visual pleasure. These greenhouses are contained, controlled perfect little worlds of their own, immune to the wind, the frost, the pests. But like Eden, these enclosed and manufactured spaces bristle with nature.

Greenhouses have existed in various guises since Roman times but it was in the 19th century that they really came into their own, with the construction of iconic glasshouses such as those at London's Kew Gardens and the Royal Greenhouses of Laeken. Often they housed vast collections of tropical specimens, colonial spoils from overseas. The Conservatory and Botanical Garden of the city of Geneva, built in 1817, is where *Botanical* began – largely by accident. One sunny evening in March 2015, seeking a calming panacea to a stressful day at work, Samuel Zeller got off the train a stop early and wandered around, randomly shooting pictures of plants that caught his eye. It was only a week later, looking through the pictures on his computer, that he saw their potential. The project has since taken him to greenhouses in Belgium, Scotland, Poland and France.

Before choosing the next greenhouse to visit, Zeller researches online, scouring pictures to identify the precise texture of glass he'll find, whether the plants are located close to the glass. Each one is its own adventure but there is a consistency to his approach. Zeller is the son of artists and a painterly influence is clear. His shots have the smudgy energy of Impressionist works by Édouard Manet and Auguste Renoir, both of whom painted greenhouses. So too is a graphic designer's eye, honed during his pre-photography career. His inclusion of the metal structure of the greenhouse creates a framing and flattening two-dimensional, canvas-like effect that plays with our sense of foreground and background. Clusters of leaves and flowers interrupt the deep blue, green-grey darkness in sudden streaks of pink, red or bright yellow. Rivulets of condensation form patterns on the glass, muck glistens golden in the sunlight.

And yet it would be a mistake to think of *Botanical* purely in terms of its aesthetics. There's a deeper message behind the series. Like our 19th century forbears, we're living through a period of rapid change, and facing an uncertain future. As seasons blur and weather conditions become more unpredictable, being able to control the climate in which we grow crops takes on a practical urgency. Across the world, people are exploring innovative ways to do this – living roofs, aquaponics systems, urban farms, greenhouse skyscrapers, even greenhouses in space . . . Scheerbart thought glass had the power to transform the world into a more beautiful, more ethical place. In Zeller's work, we see the glasshouse as a thing of wonder, but also a symbol of hope – of human ingenuity working hand-in-hand with nature.

PHOTOGRAPHER'S NOTE

by Samuel Zeller

I remember the days spent at my grandma's farm collecting and observing plants and insects, the walks in the mountains with my dad, the long tours at the museums with my mum. There was no smartphone, no TV and no internet.

The apartment with the fireplace and the garden changed to a smaller flat on a busy street, the farm was sold and new constructions began on the sides of the valley, roads were built in the woods. Studies came and went as years flew by. I was then immersed in an ultra-connected world full of deadlines, emails and complex projects. Work, sleep and repeat. I almost forgot about my childlike way of seeing the world.

Then, in 2015, on the way home after a particularly bad day at the office in Geneva, I got off the train a stop early to visit the botanical garden. My anger and anxiety heightened my sensitivity. In that green island inside the city I discovered what I saw as a series of paintings behind the glass, a refracted reality. I took the first 10 photographs of the project that day.

A year after my visit to the garden I said goodbye to my career as a designer, realising that photography was the best tool I had against the crazy rhythm of our society.

I've travelled to many different places in Europe, aiming to seek out those glimpses of nature protected from the elements. It took me 26 years to understand how fragile life can be and how important it is for us to slow down and do what we love.

I guess that all good things take time to grow.

ACKNOWLEDGEMENTS

I would like to express my gratitude to the people who have helped me make this book a reality; to those who provided support, accommodation, invaluable feedback, recommendations and assisted in the editing and design.

Thank you to Cris Jiménez and Jose Calero, Mike and Toni Andrews, and Anaëlle Raguet for kindly hosting me during my travels. Thank you to Anna for showing me around Warsaw and Adriana for your time in Poland. Thank you Andreia for the incredible time spent with you in Portugal.

Thanks to Sylvester Zagato for taking the time to identify and put a name on the plants visible in the book. Thank you to Viviane, Denise and Méline for giving your feedback on the first layout.

A big thank you to the photographers who I regularly converse with, who have always supported me in my personal projects: Craig Whitehead, Peter Clarkson, Alex Rodriguez and Niels Ackermann. A special thank you to Zara Meduna for taking a portrait of me in Prague.

Last but not least: thank you to Martin, Ann and the incredible team at Hoxton Mini Press for believing in my work and pushing me to extend the initial project. Thank you Friederike for your impeccable sense of aesthetics and your help in the final sequencing of this book. I beg my forgiveness for those whose names I have failed to mention.

This book is dedicated to my dad Eric. I know you would be proud.

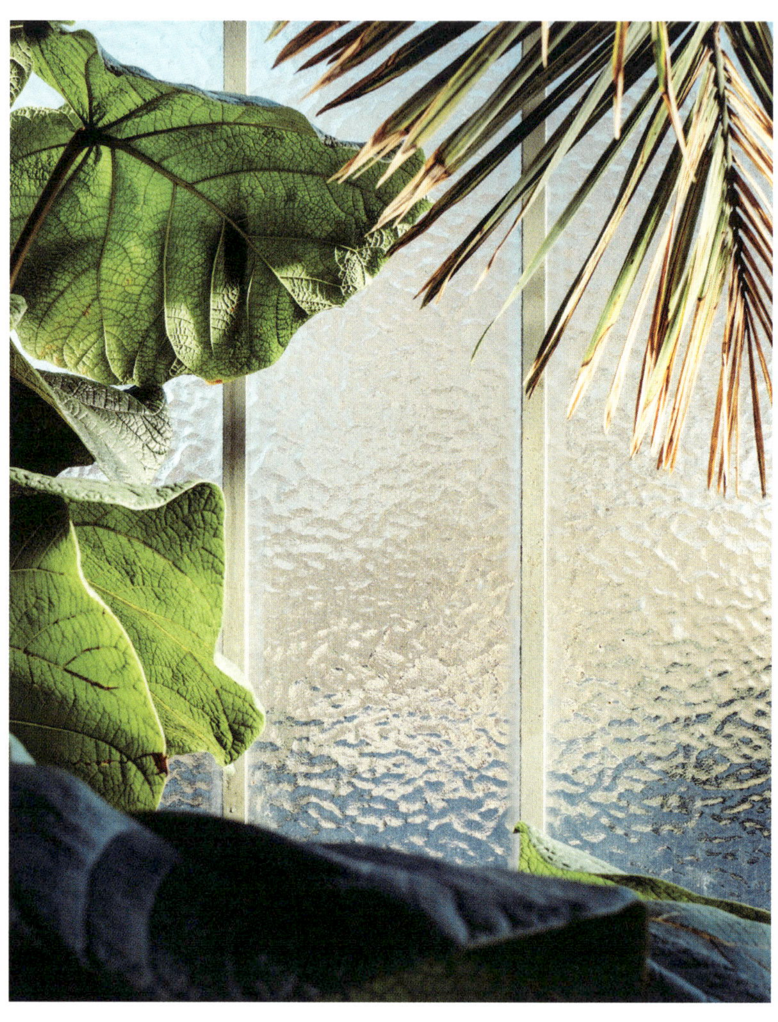

Geneva, Switzerland *(above & opposite)*
Amsterdam, Netherlands *(overleaf)*

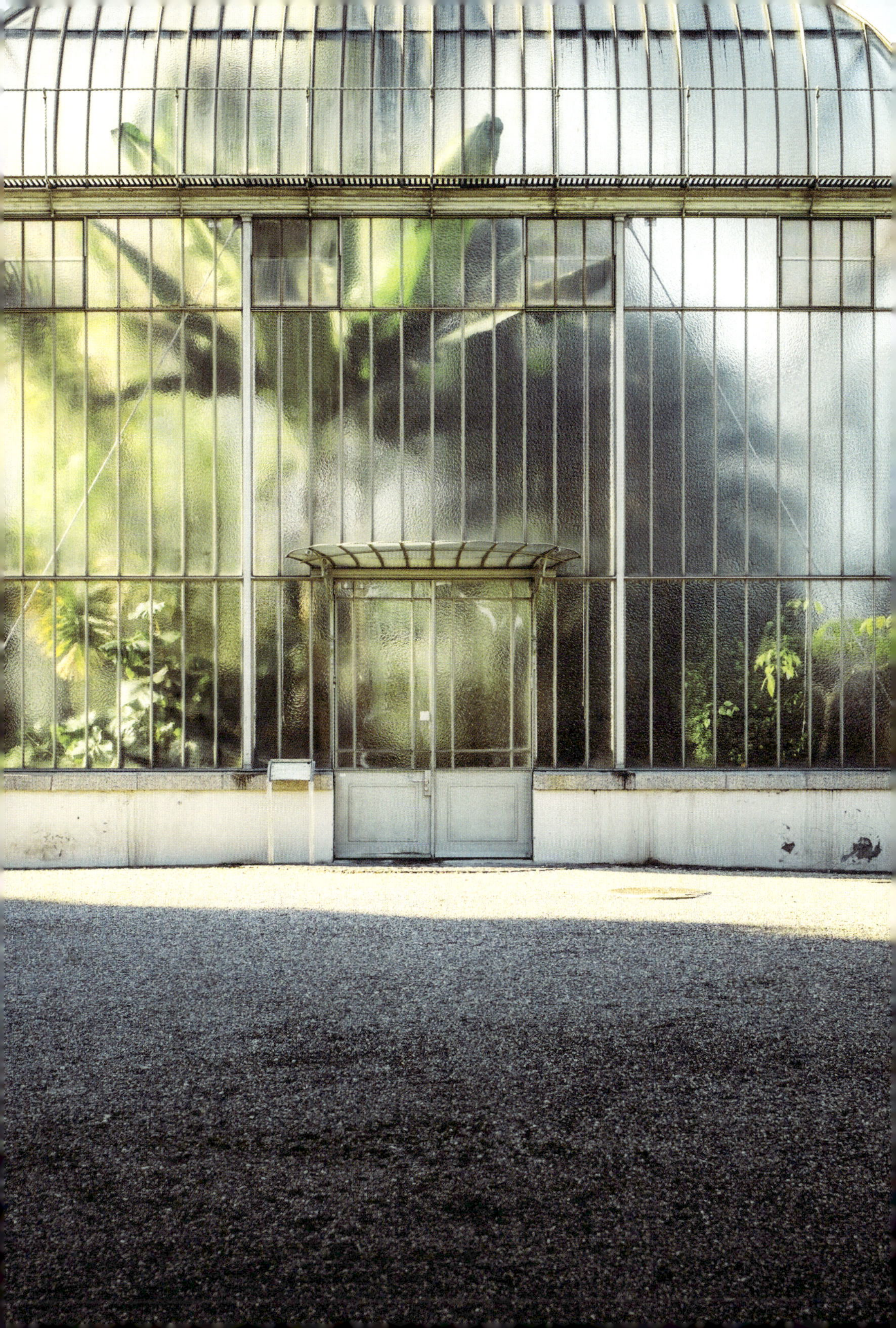

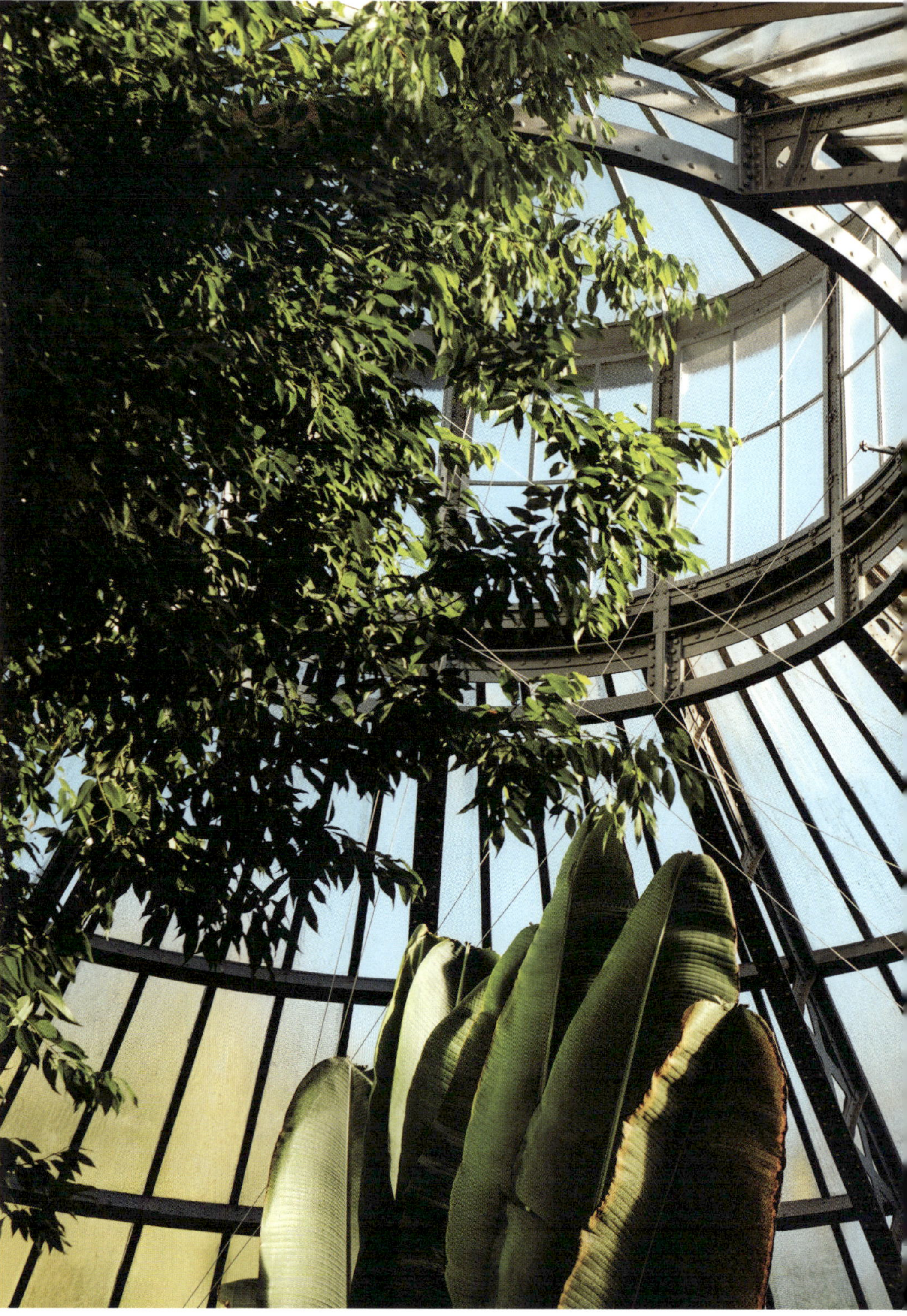

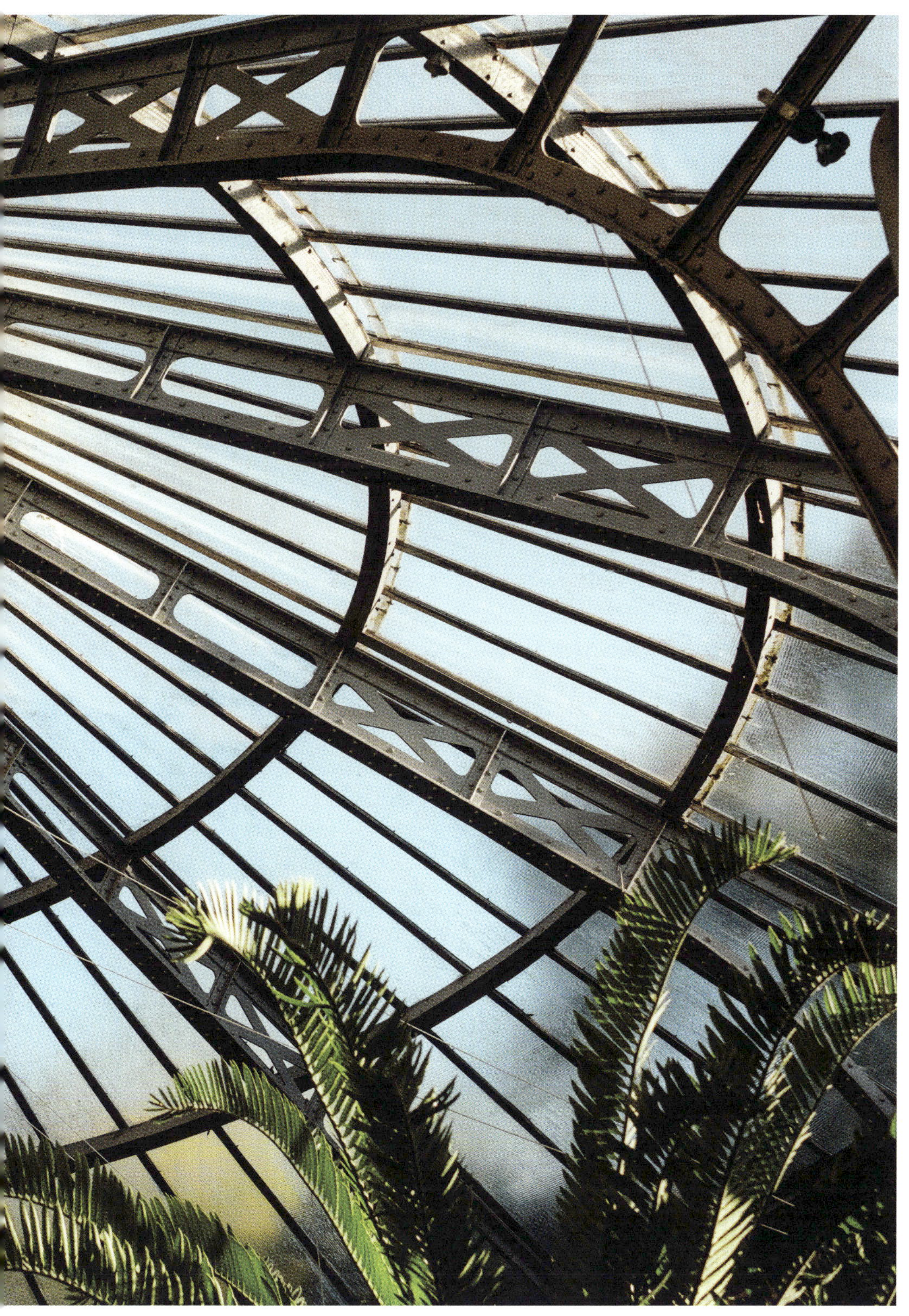

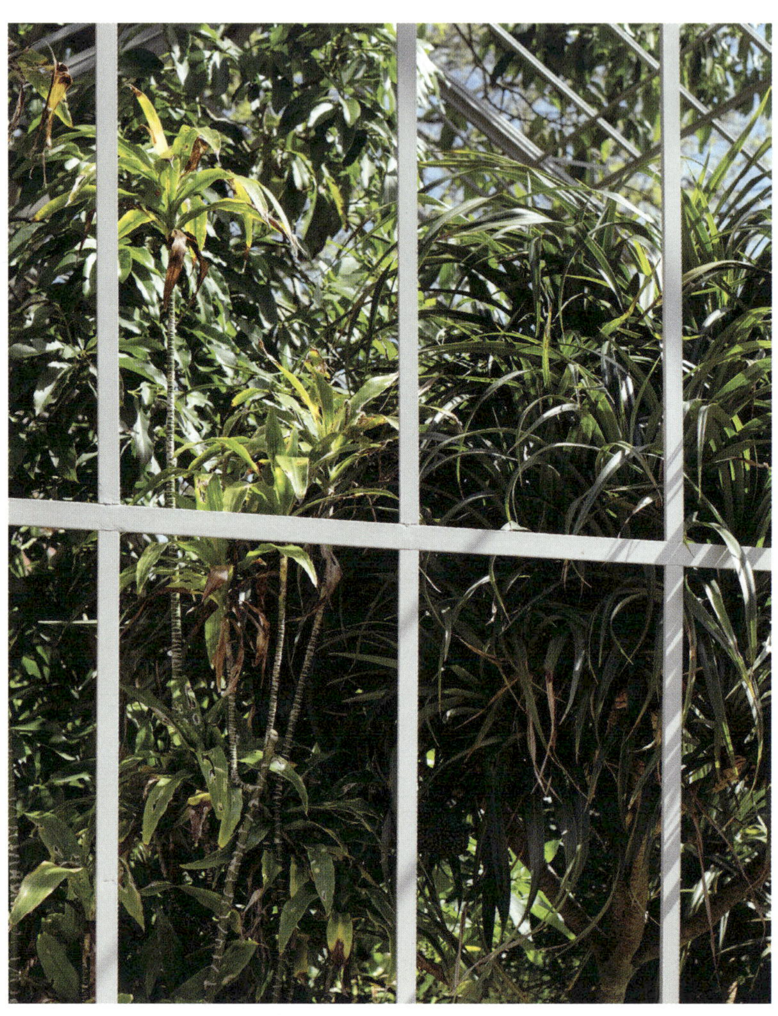

  Porto, Portugal *(above)* Glasgow, Scotland *(opposite)*

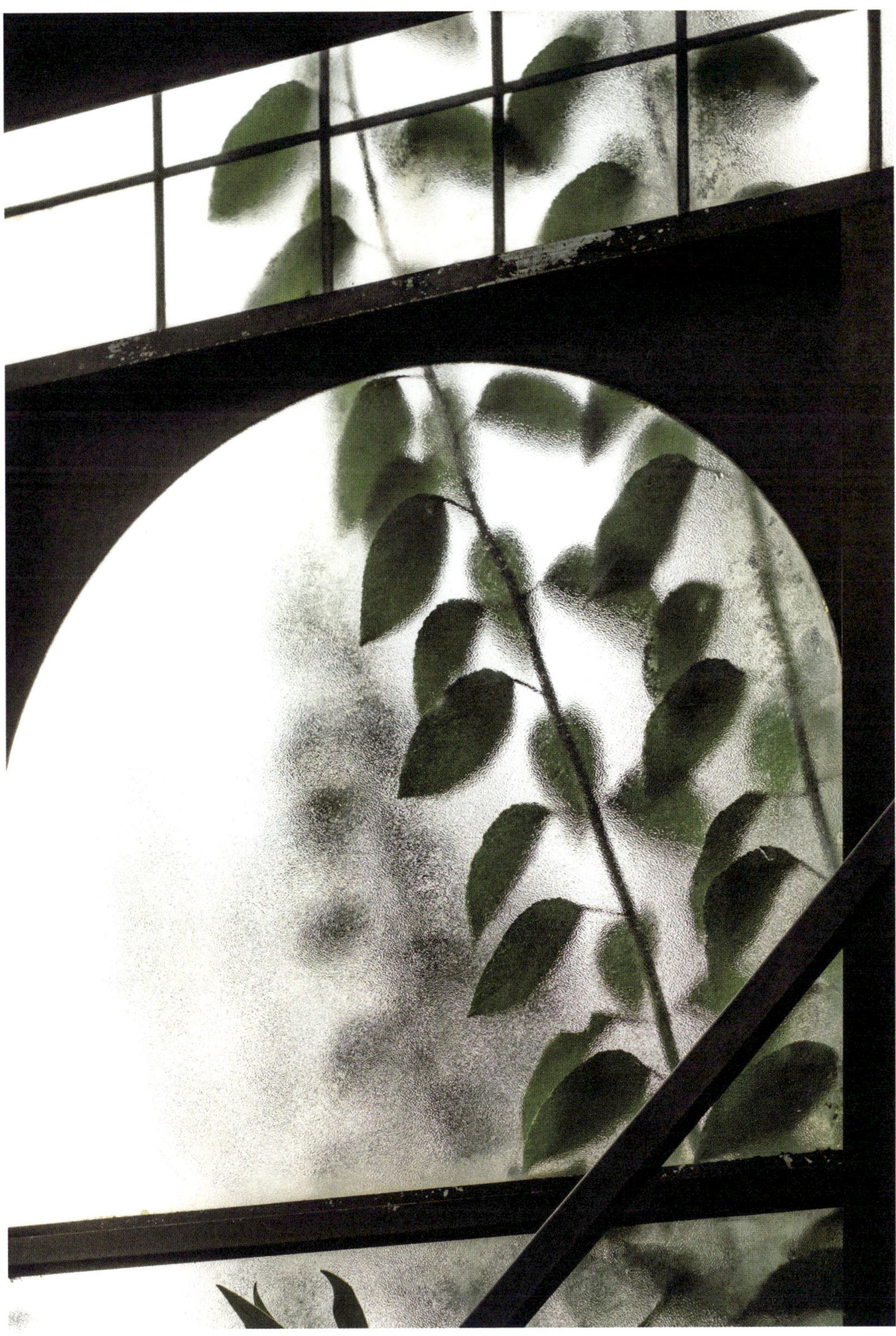

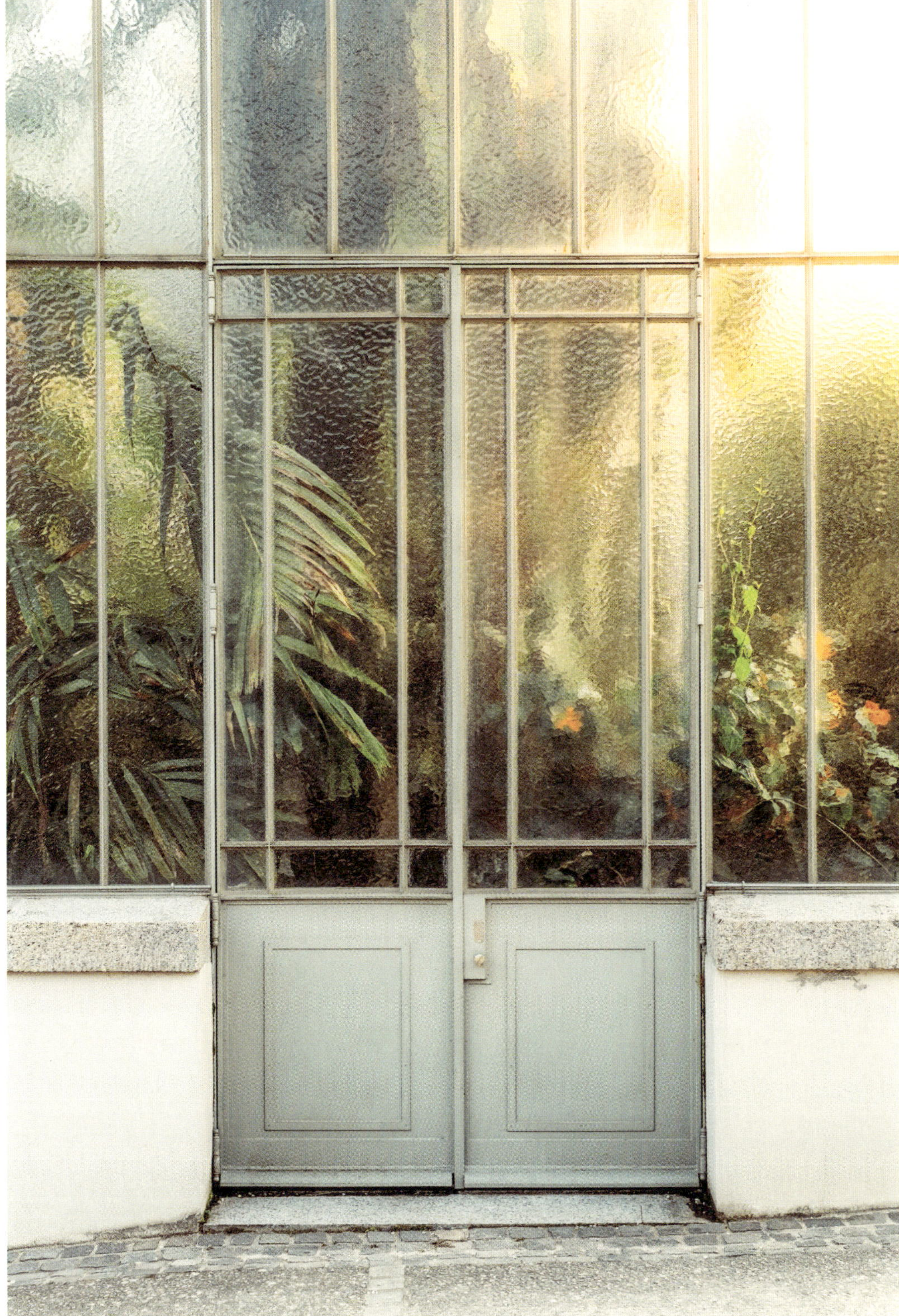

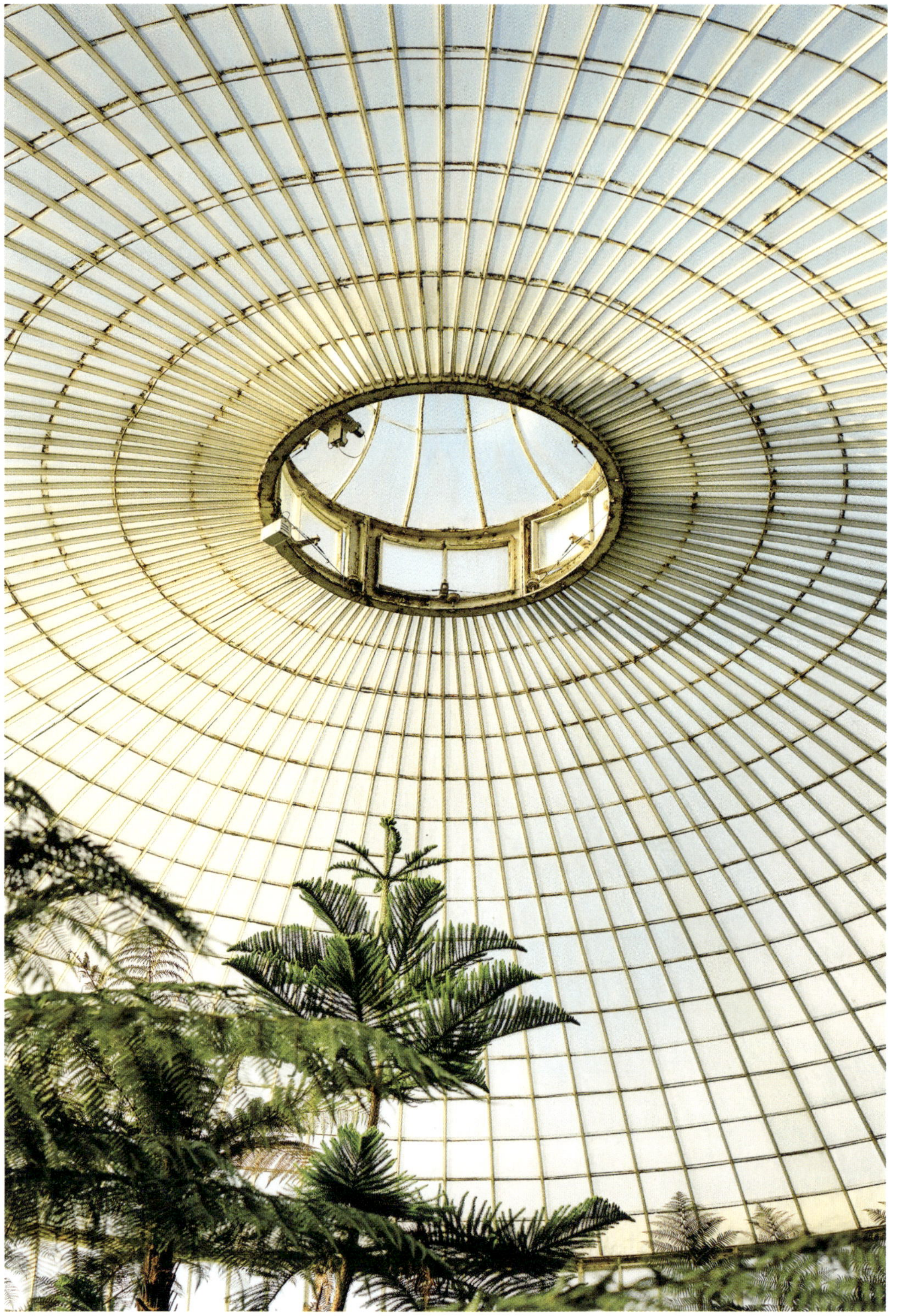

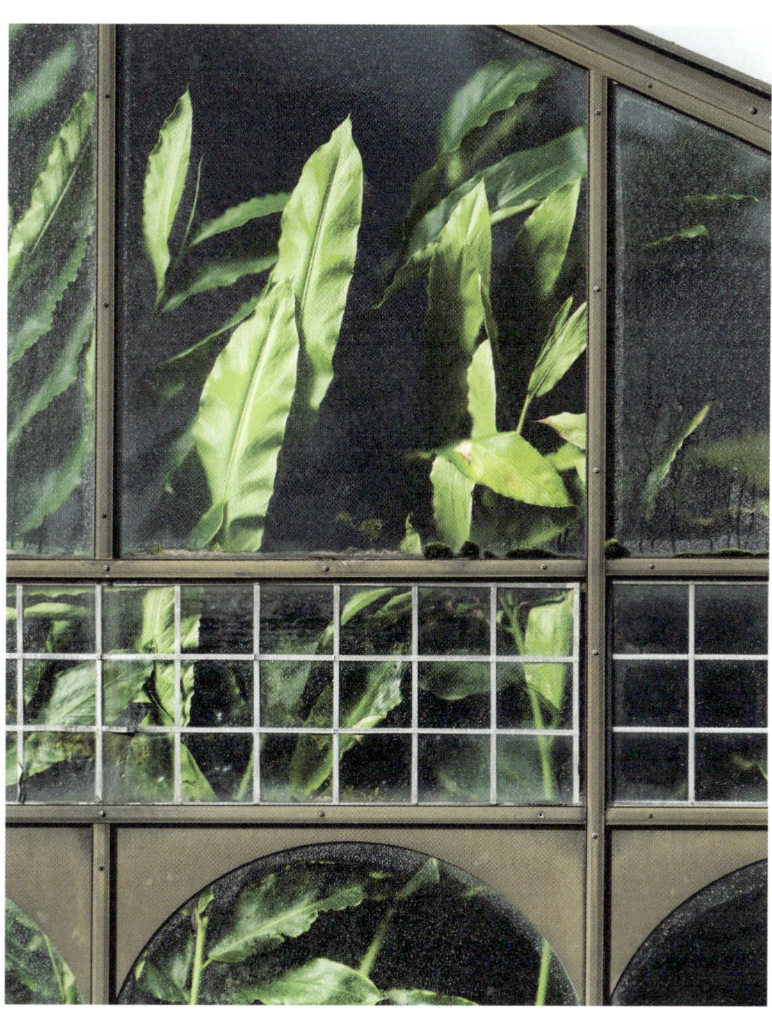

21   Glasgow, Scotland (*opposite, above & overleaf*)

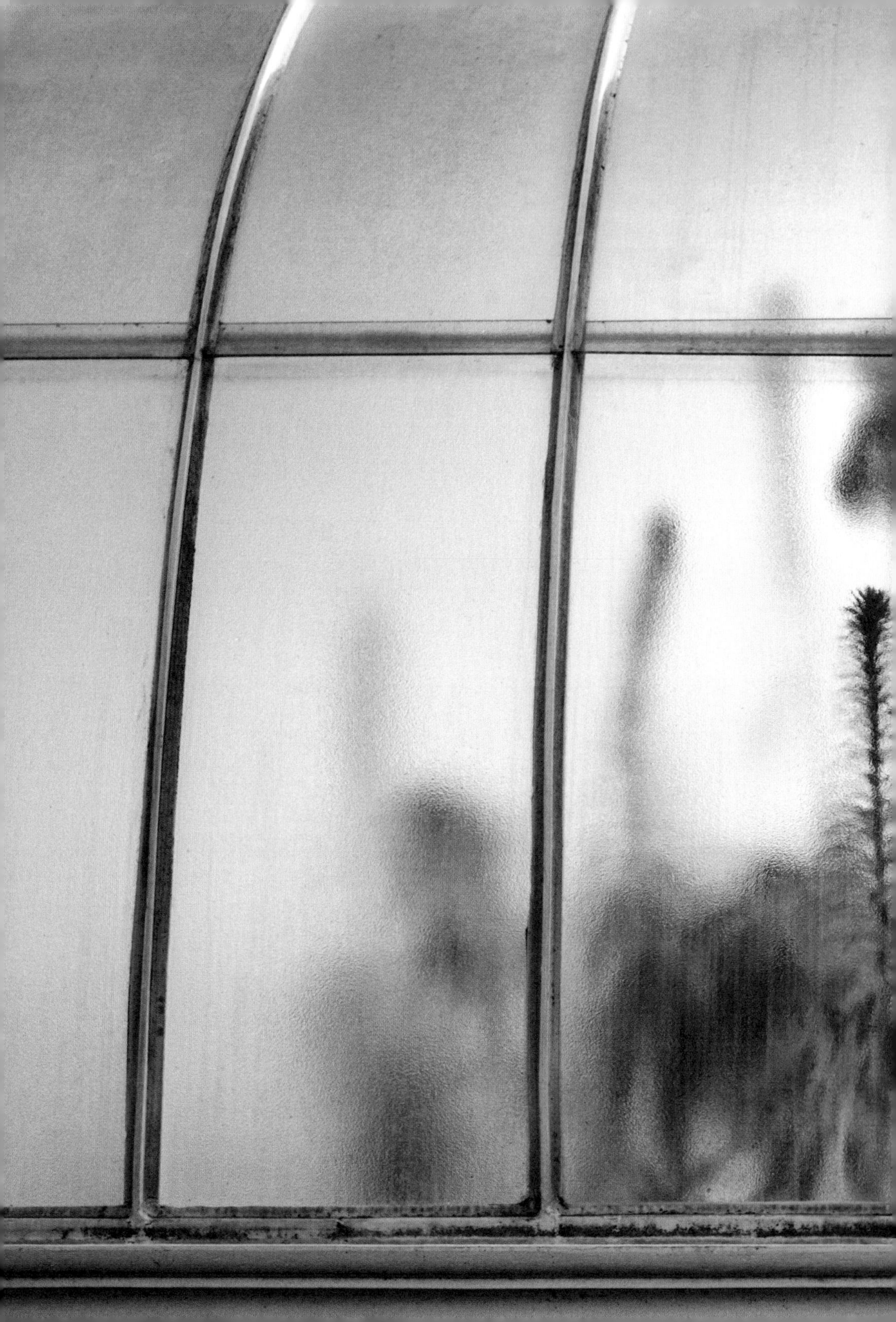

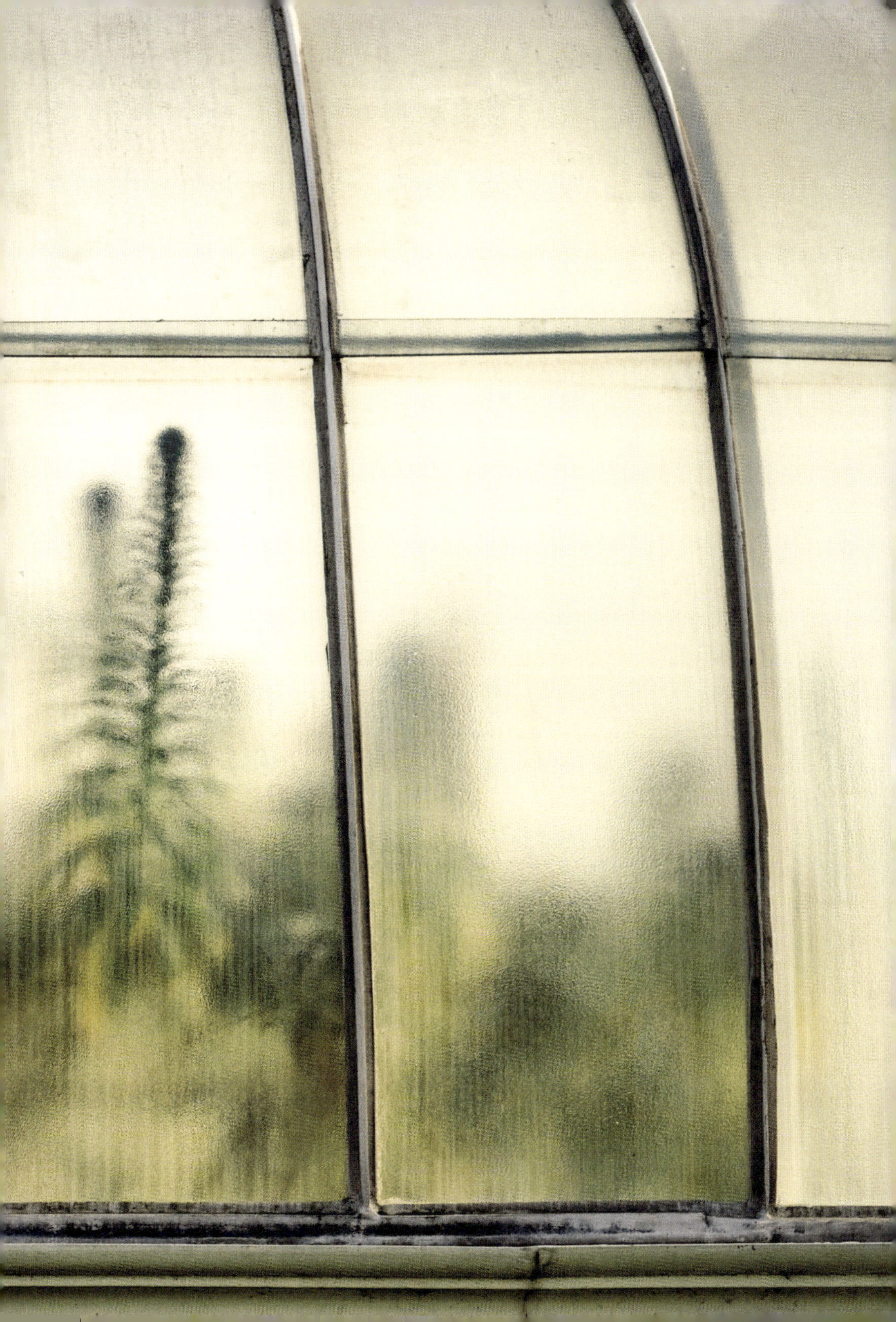

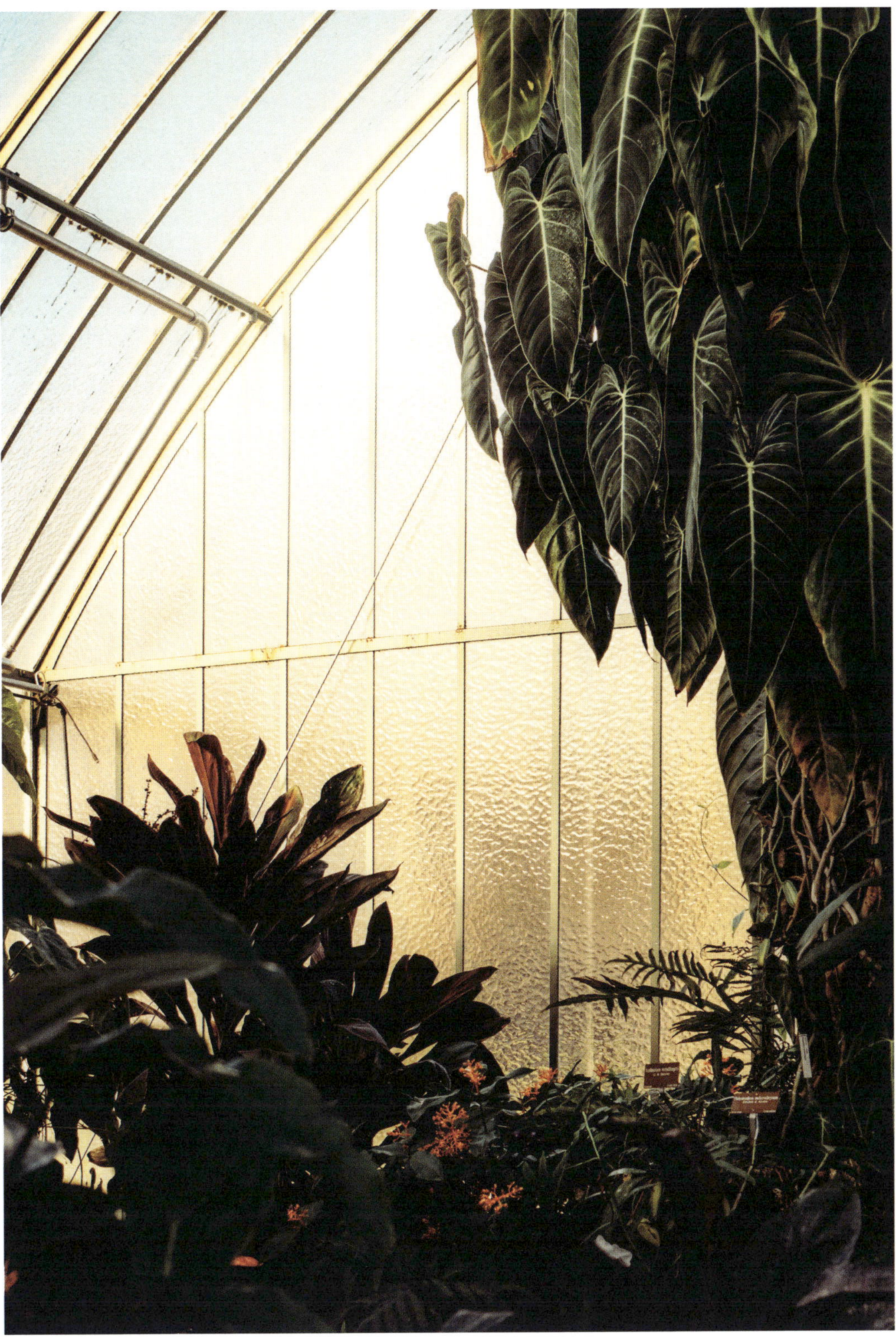

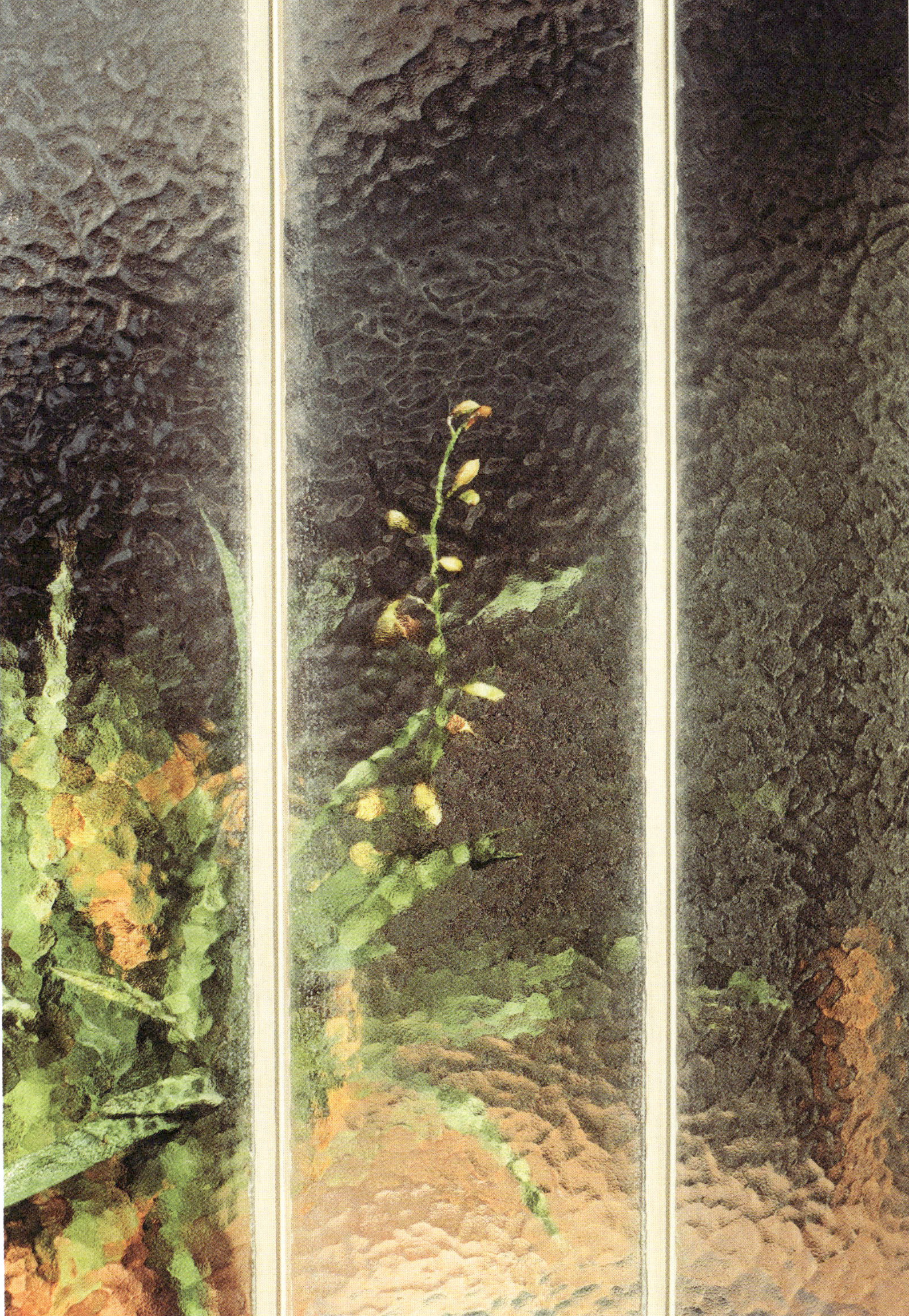

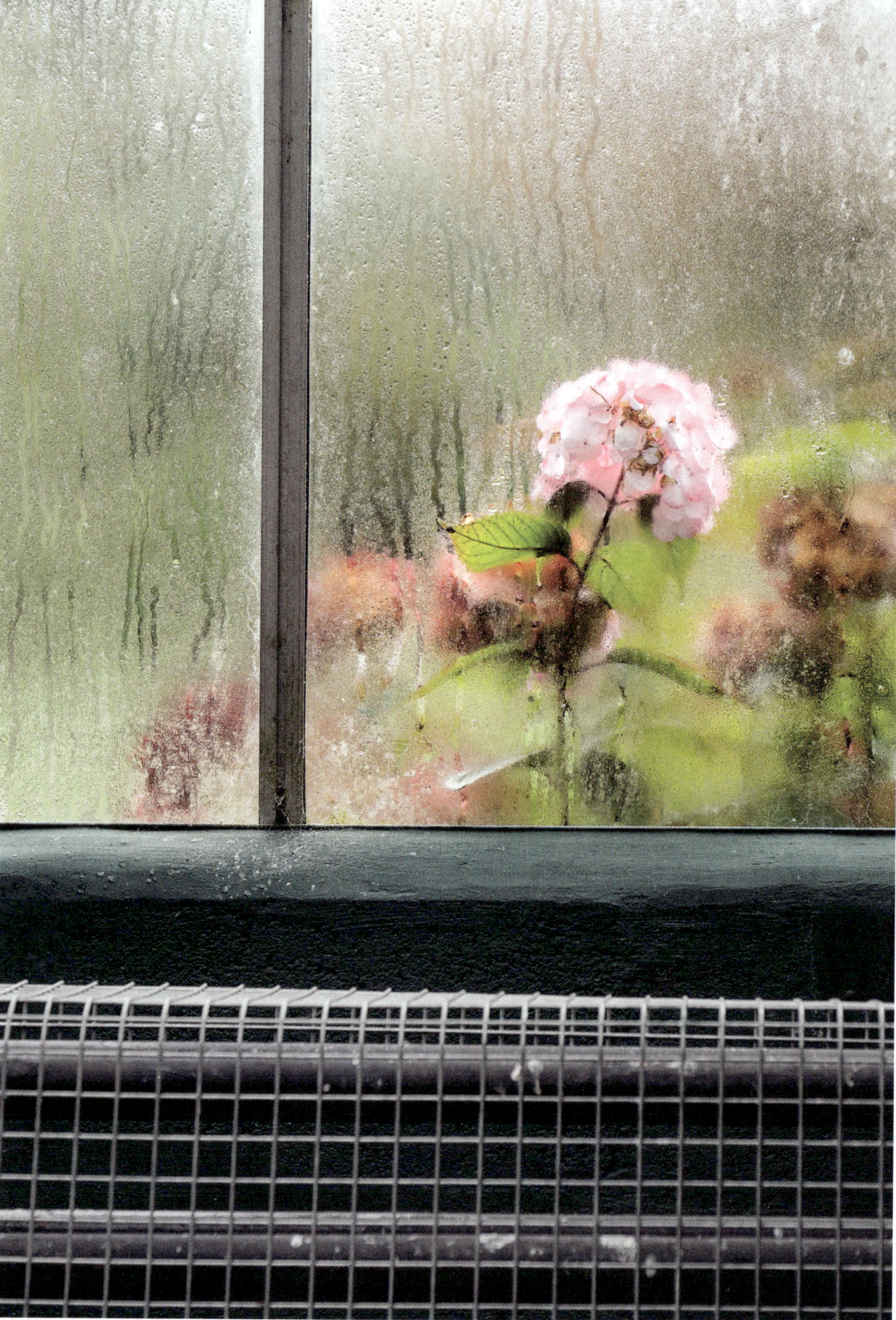

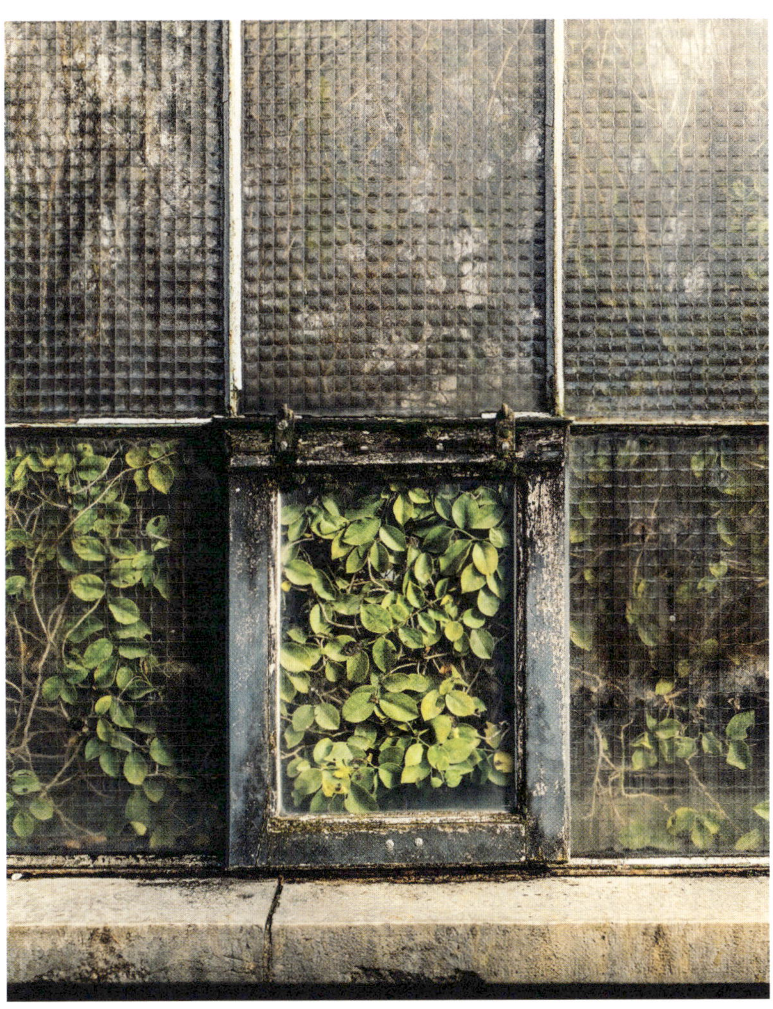

29   Dundee, Scotland *(opposite)* Lyon, France *(above)*

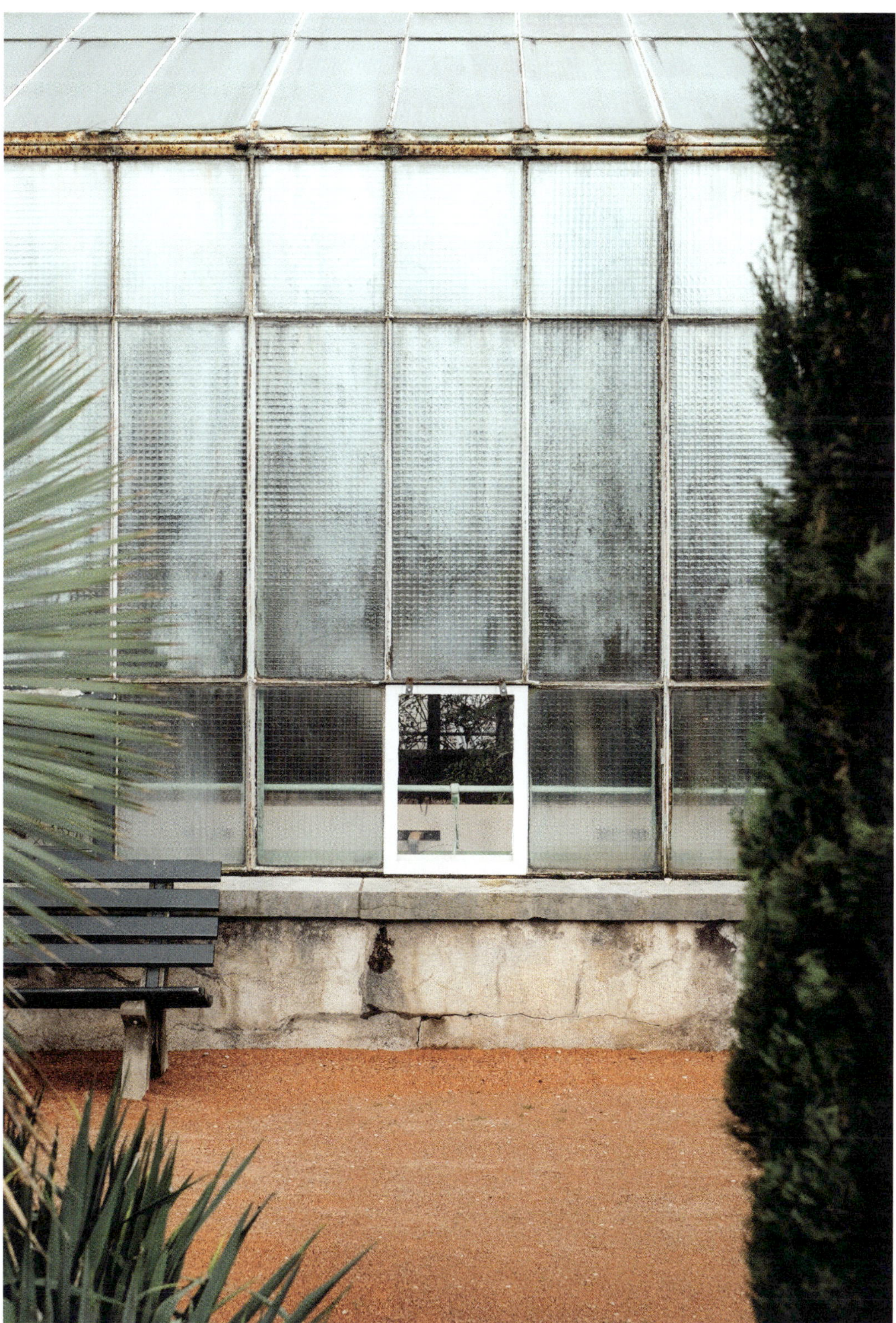

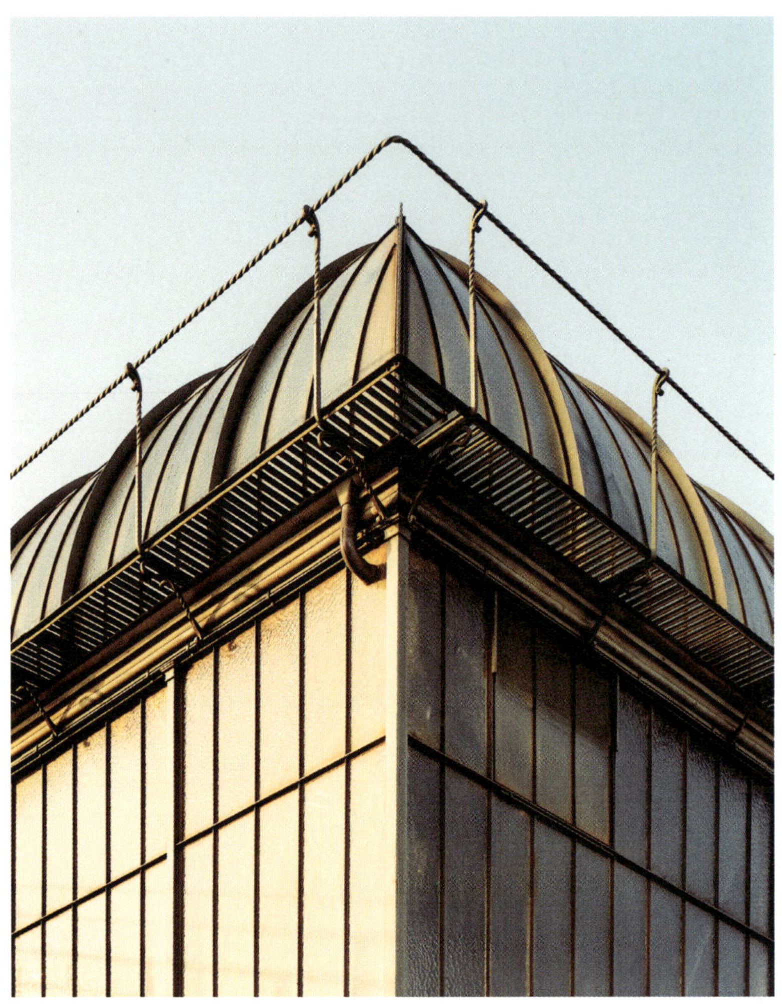

32   Geneva, Switzerland

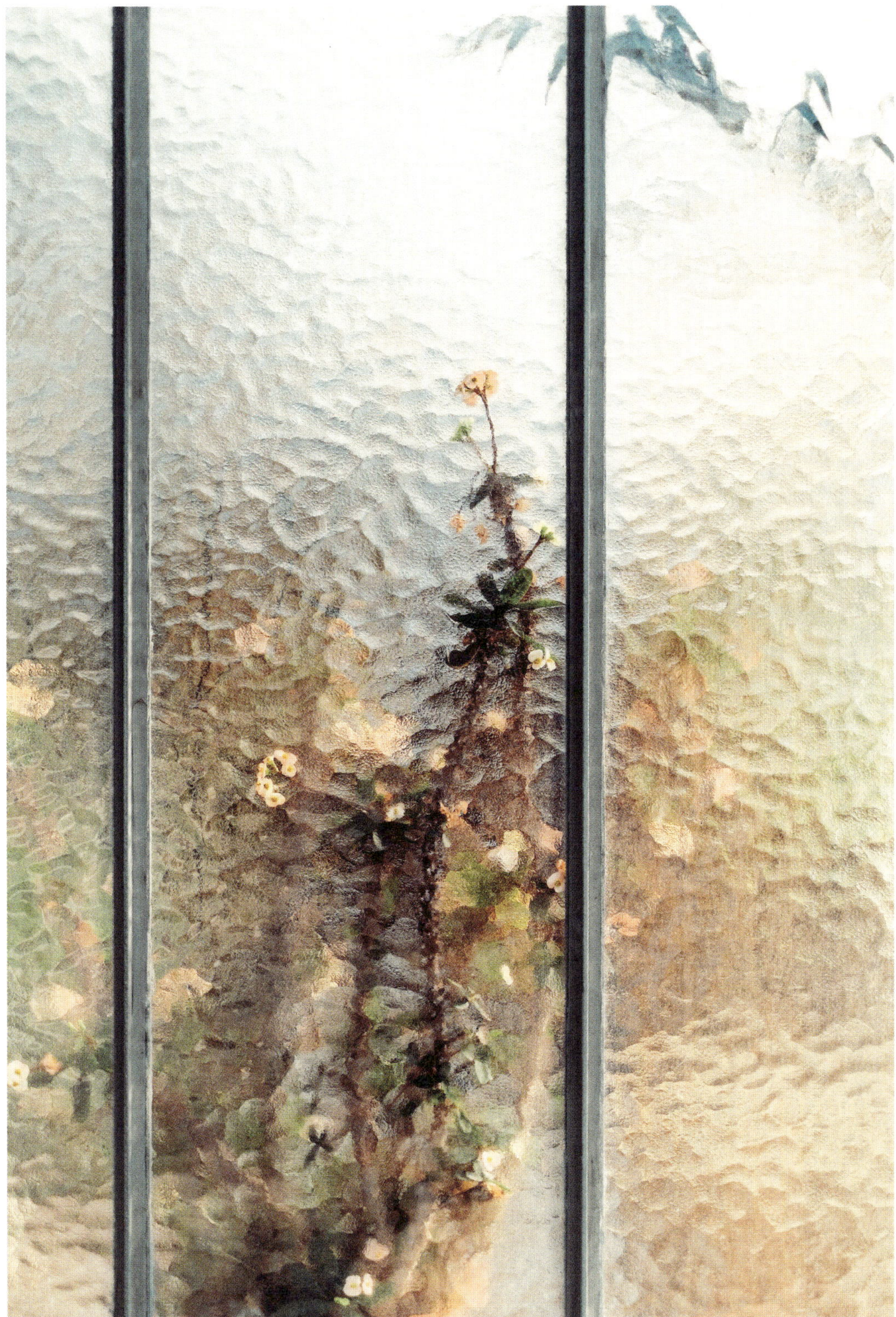

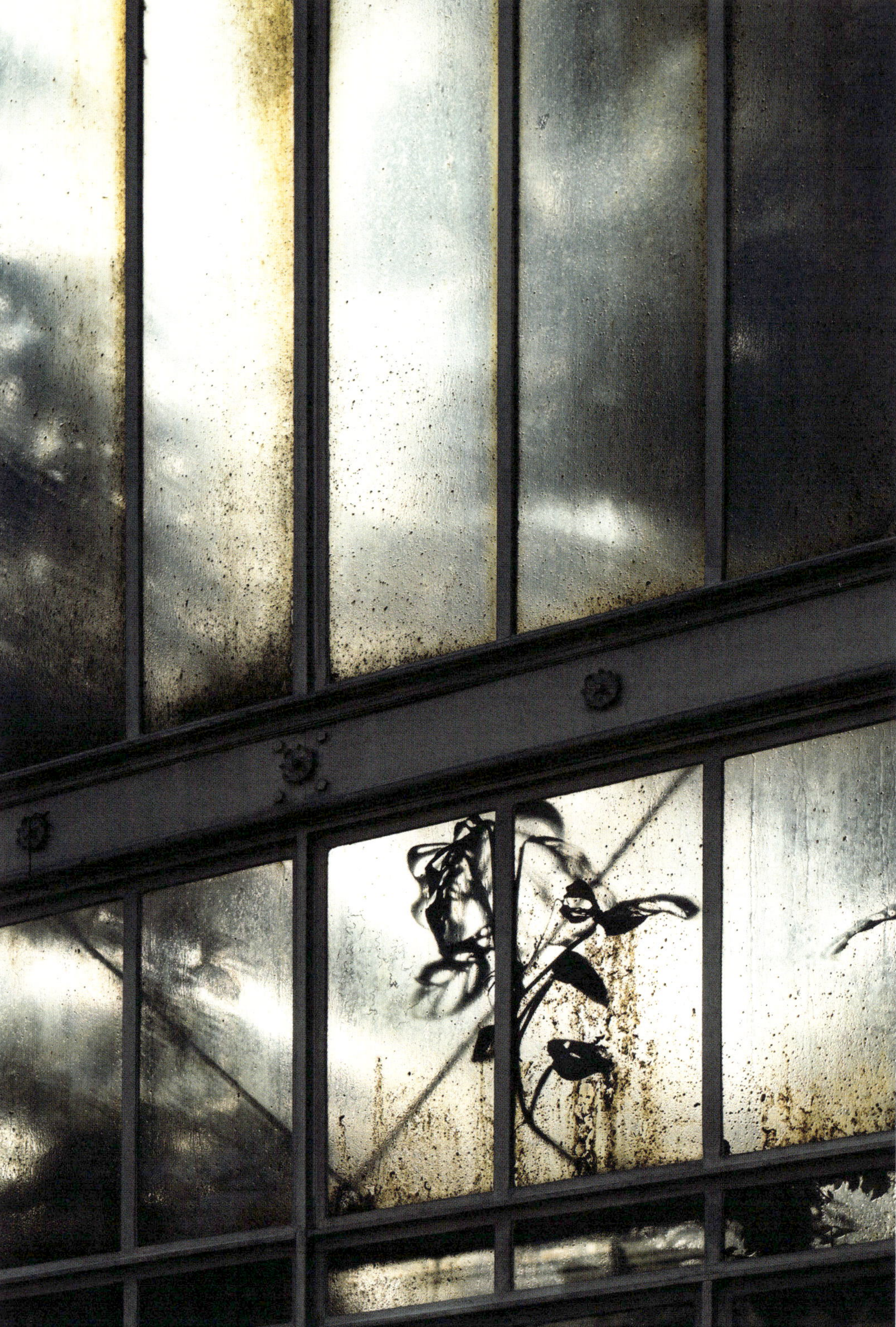

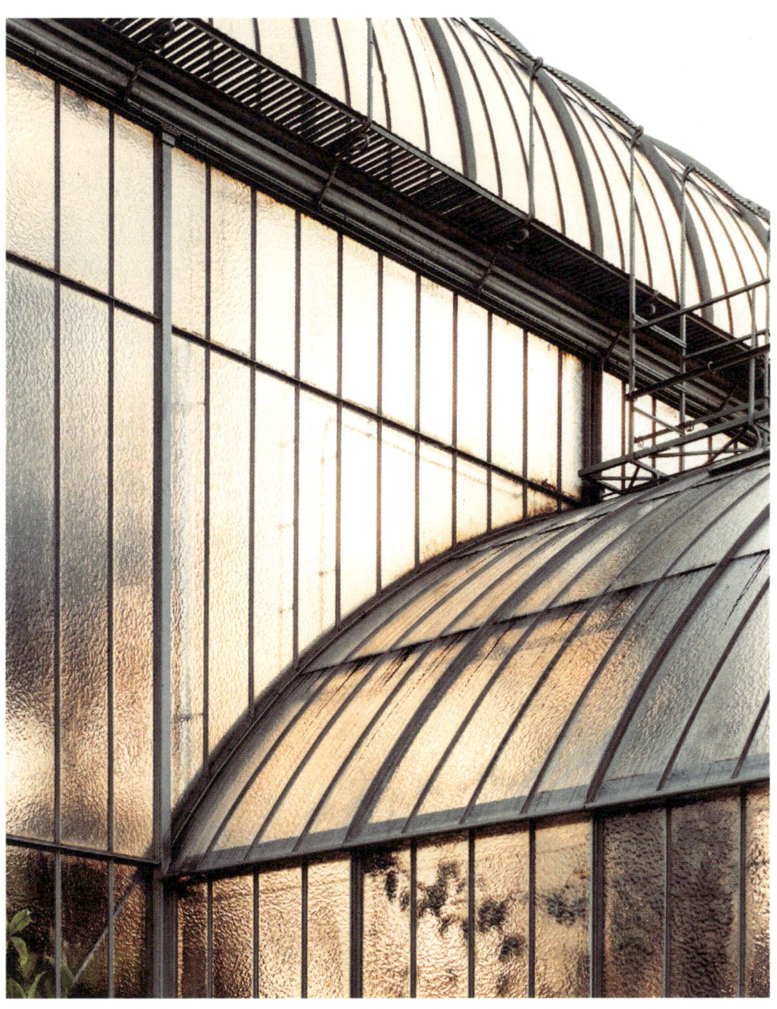

   Nantes, France *(opposite)* Geneva, Switzerland *(above)*

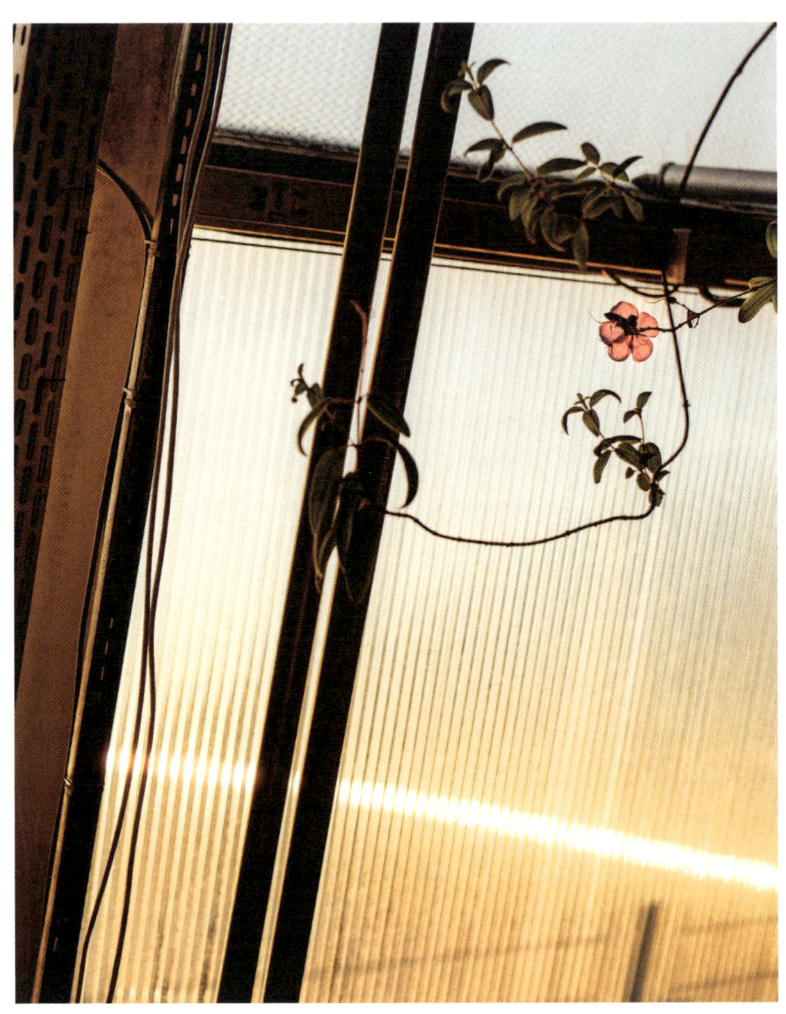

36   Prague, Czech Republic (*above*) Geneva, Switzerland (*opposite*)

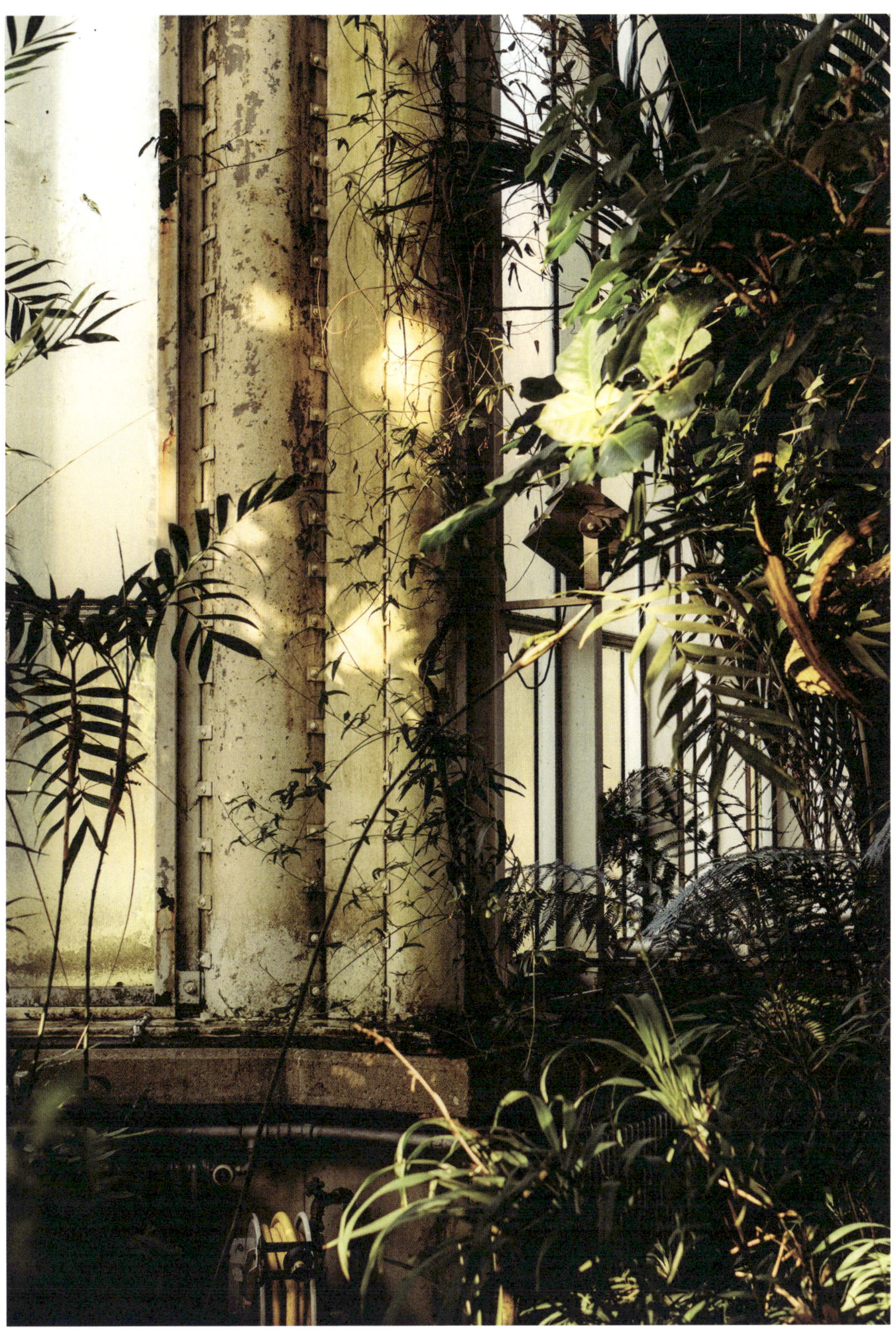

     Geneva, Switzerland *(opposite & overleaf)*

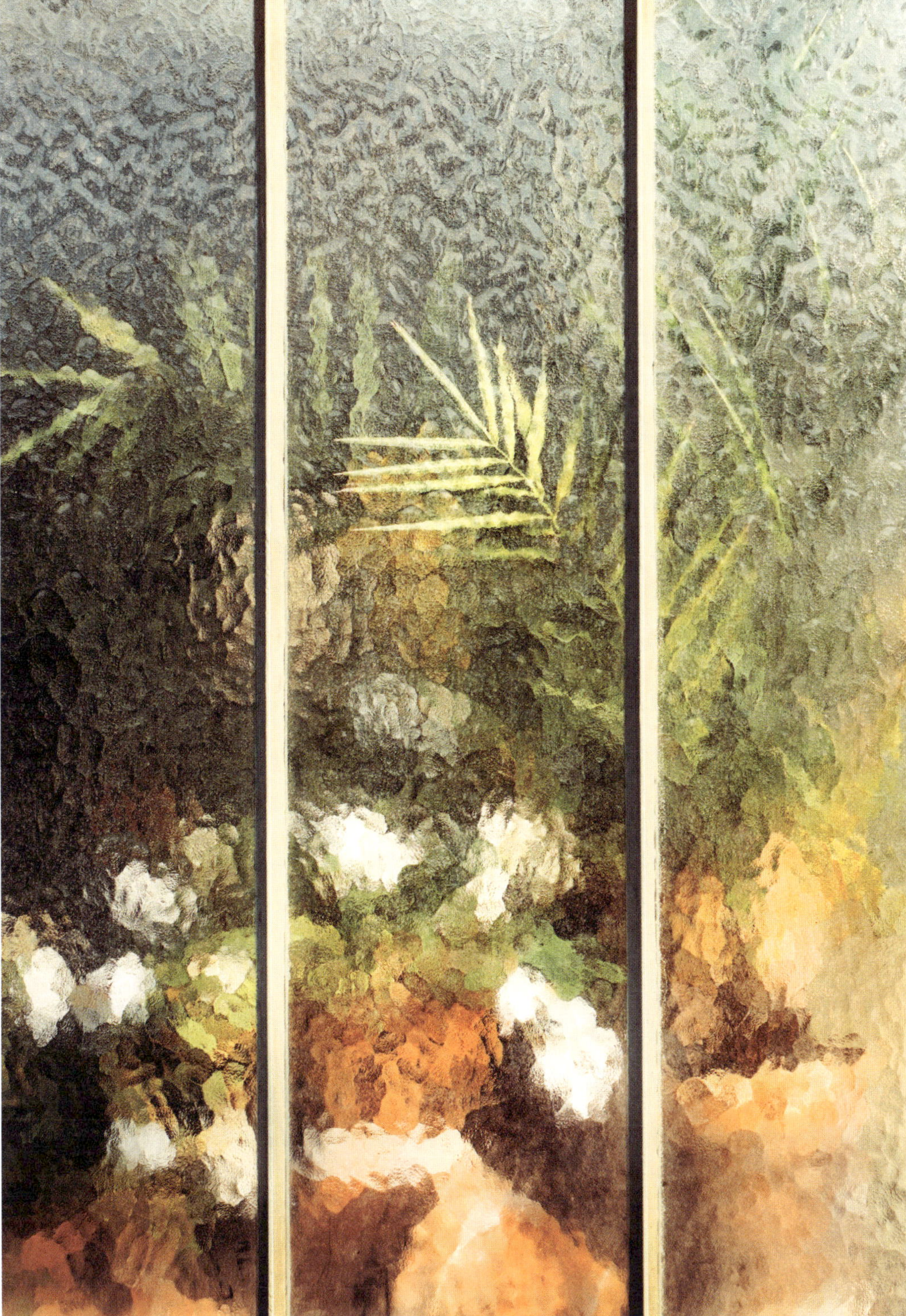

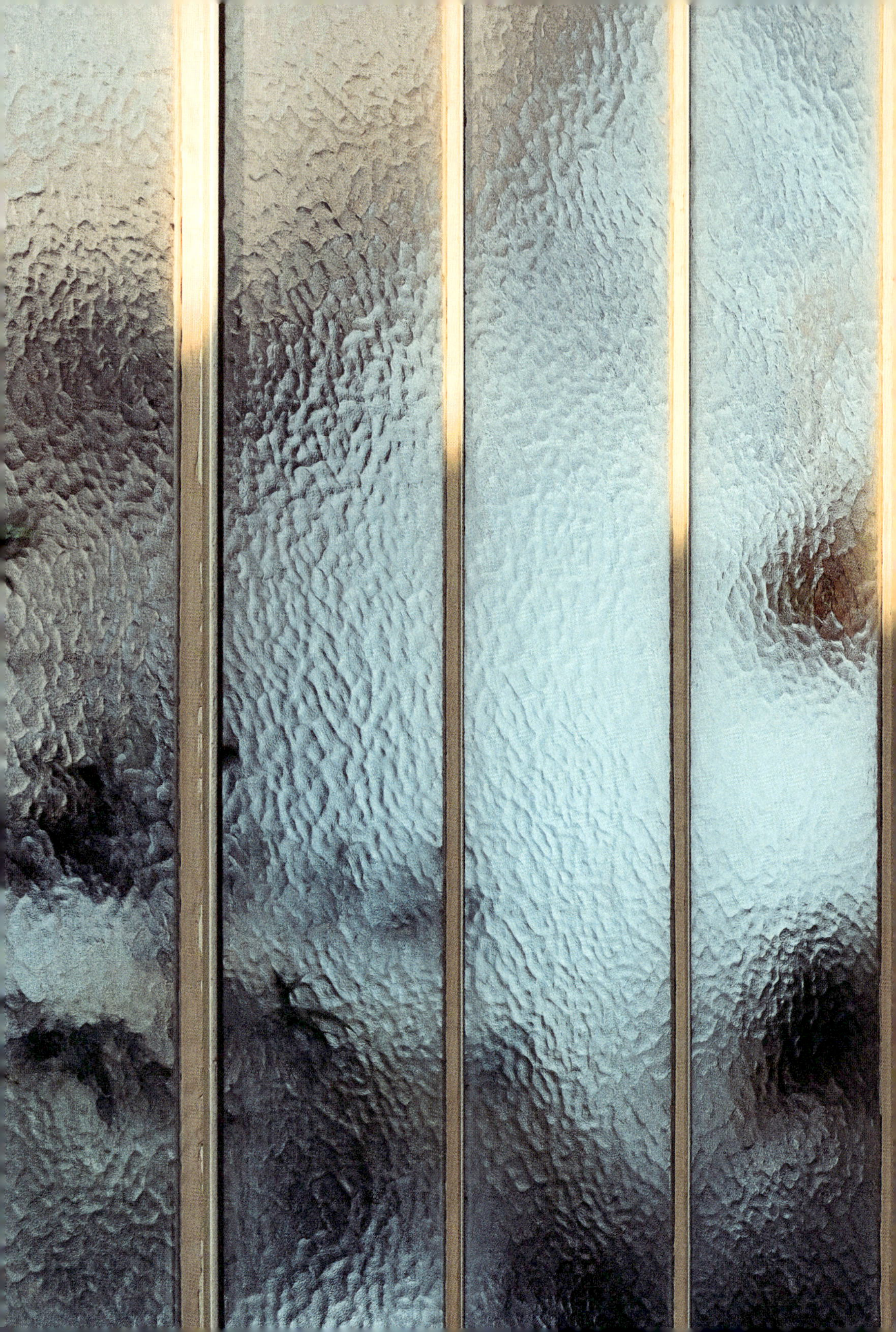

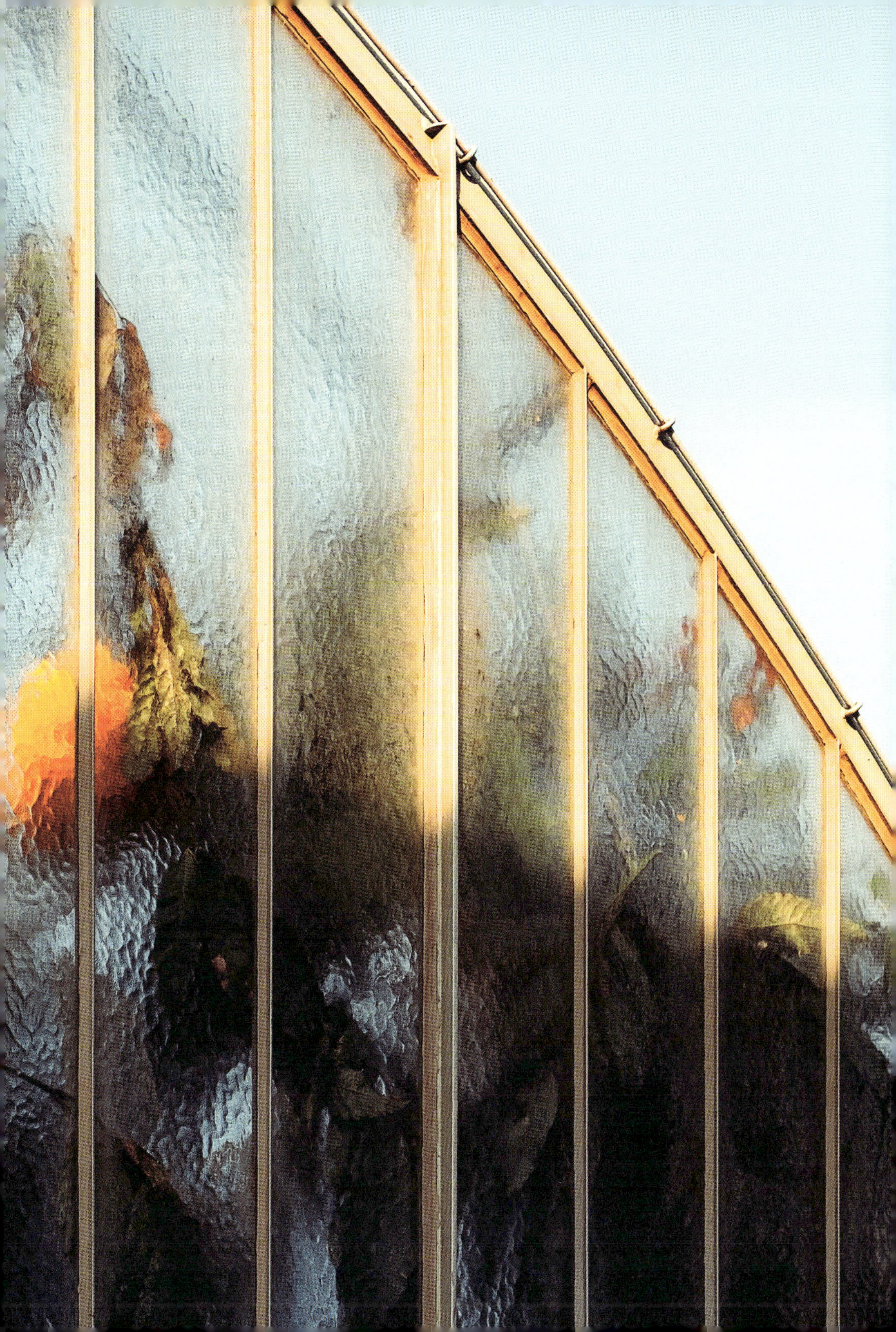

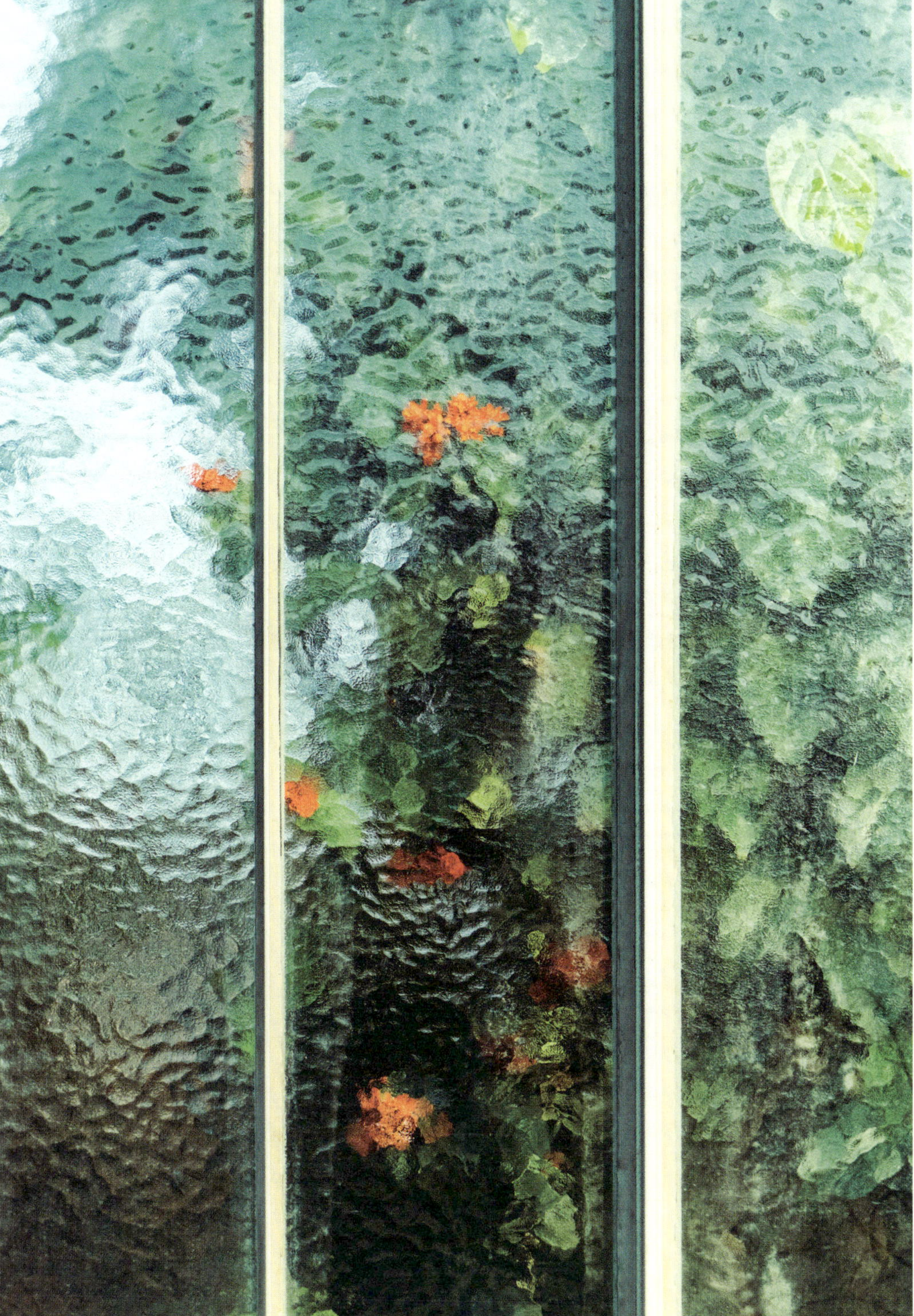

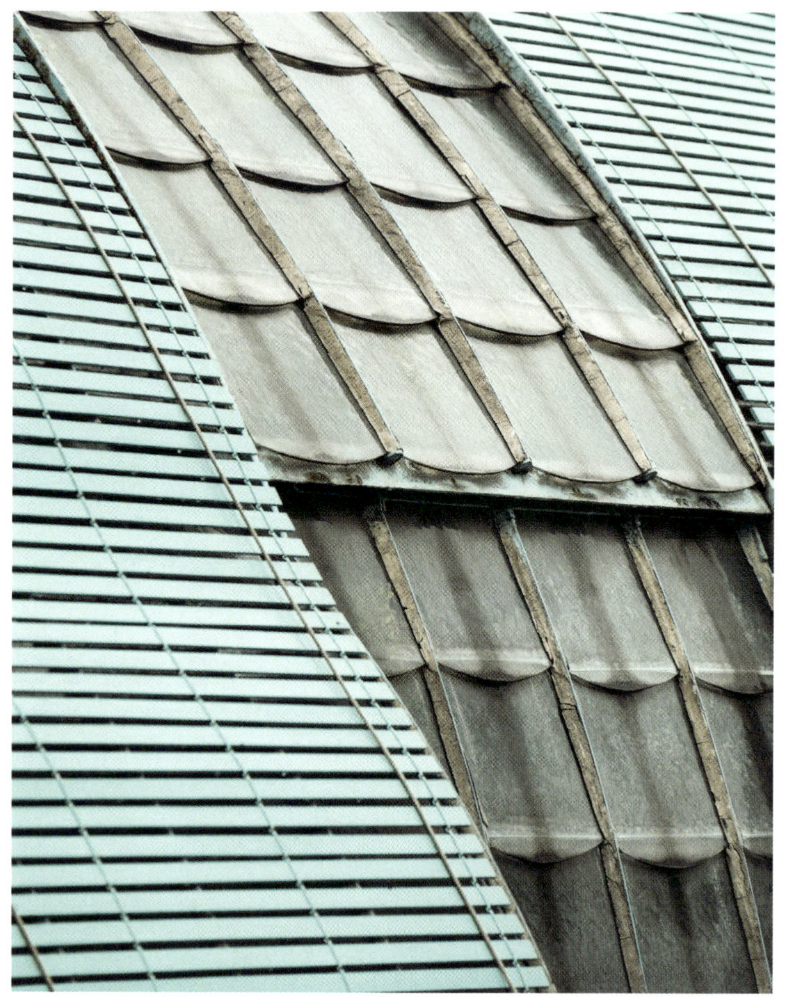

     Paris, France

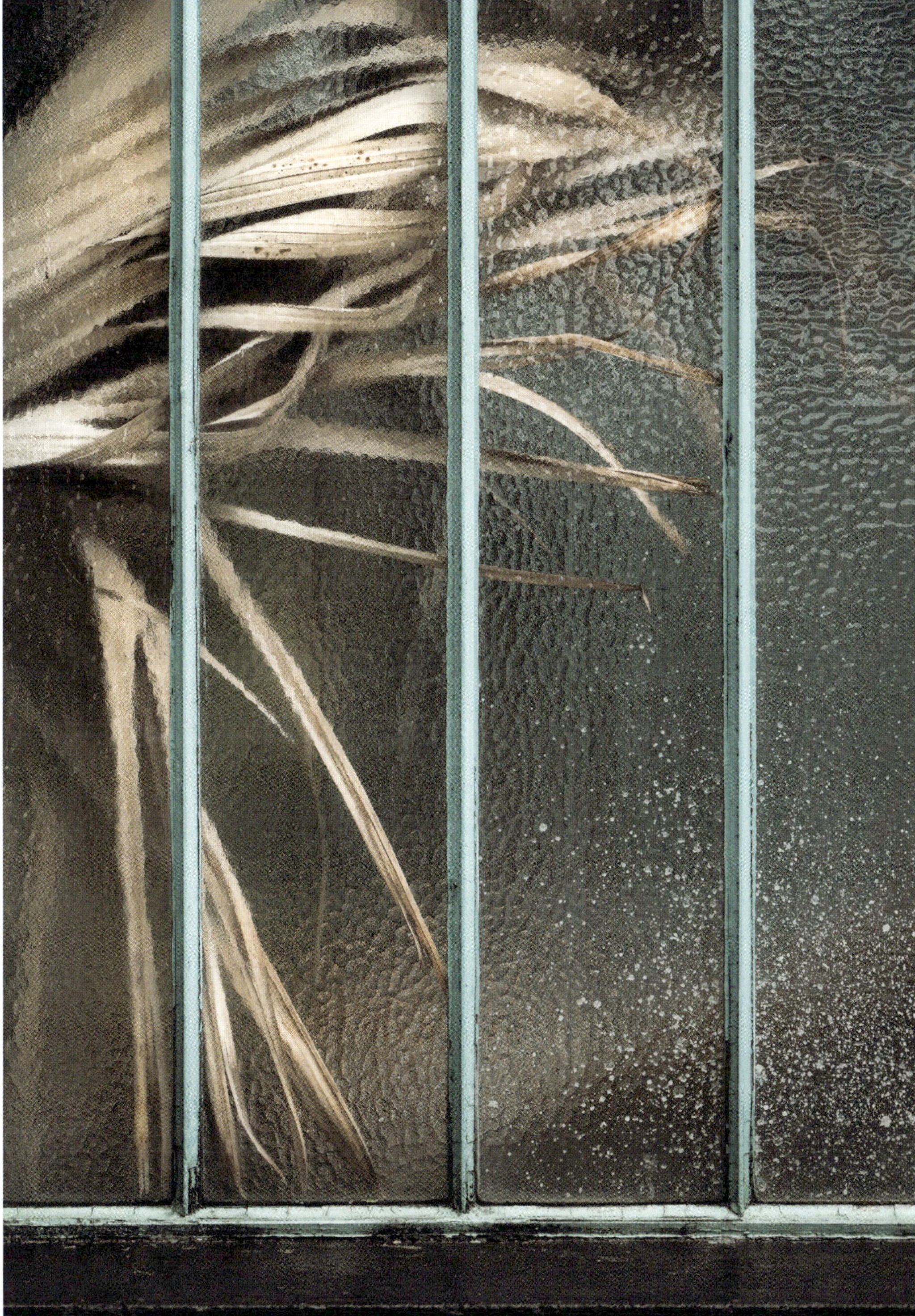

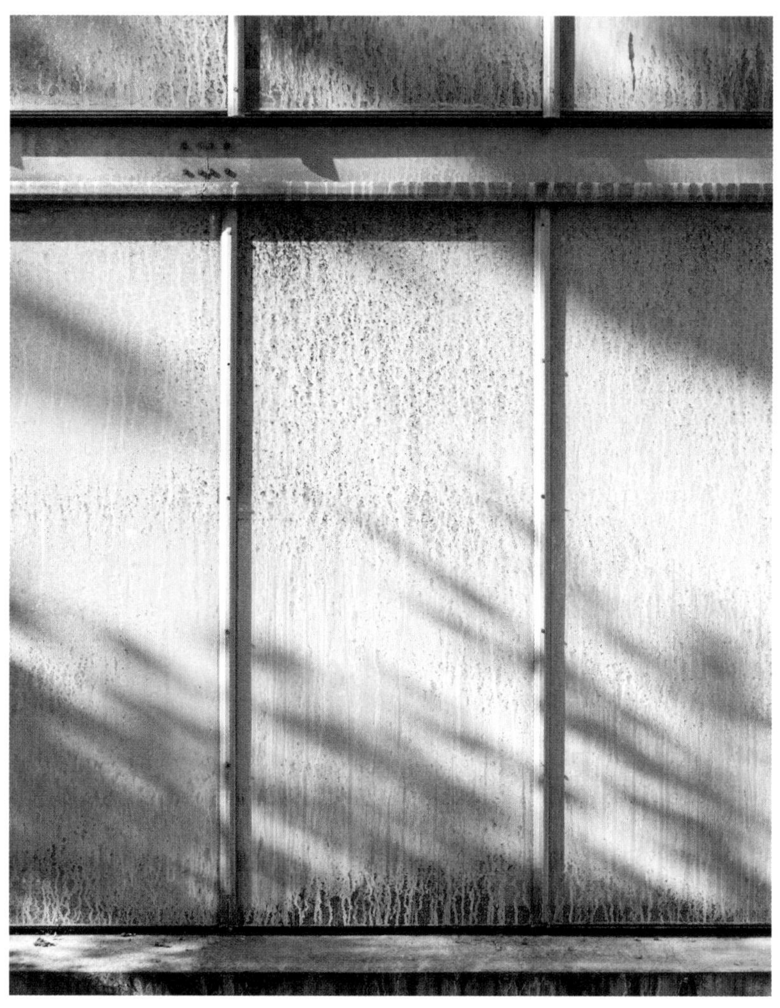

      Poznań, Poland *(above)* Nantes, France *(opposite)*

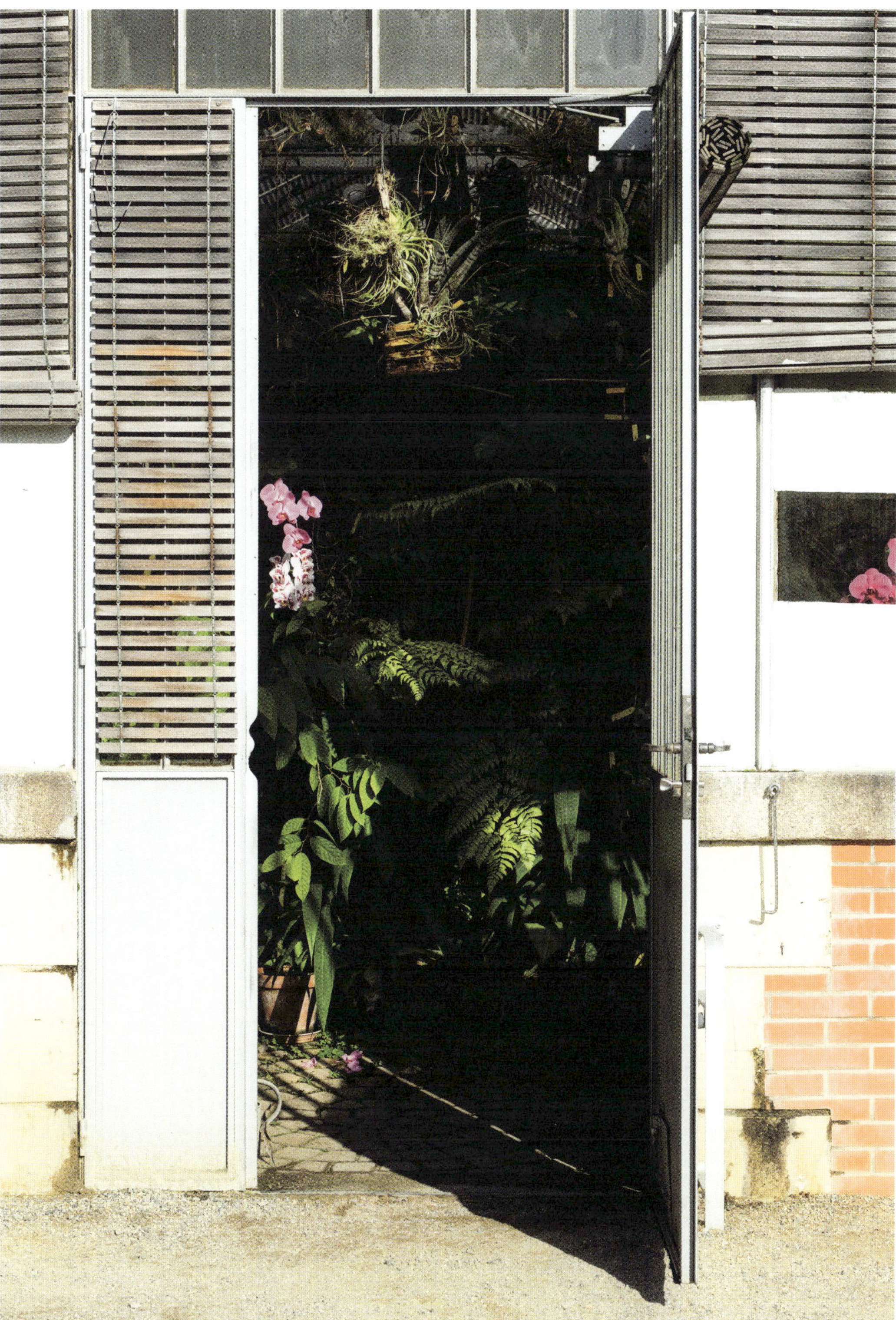

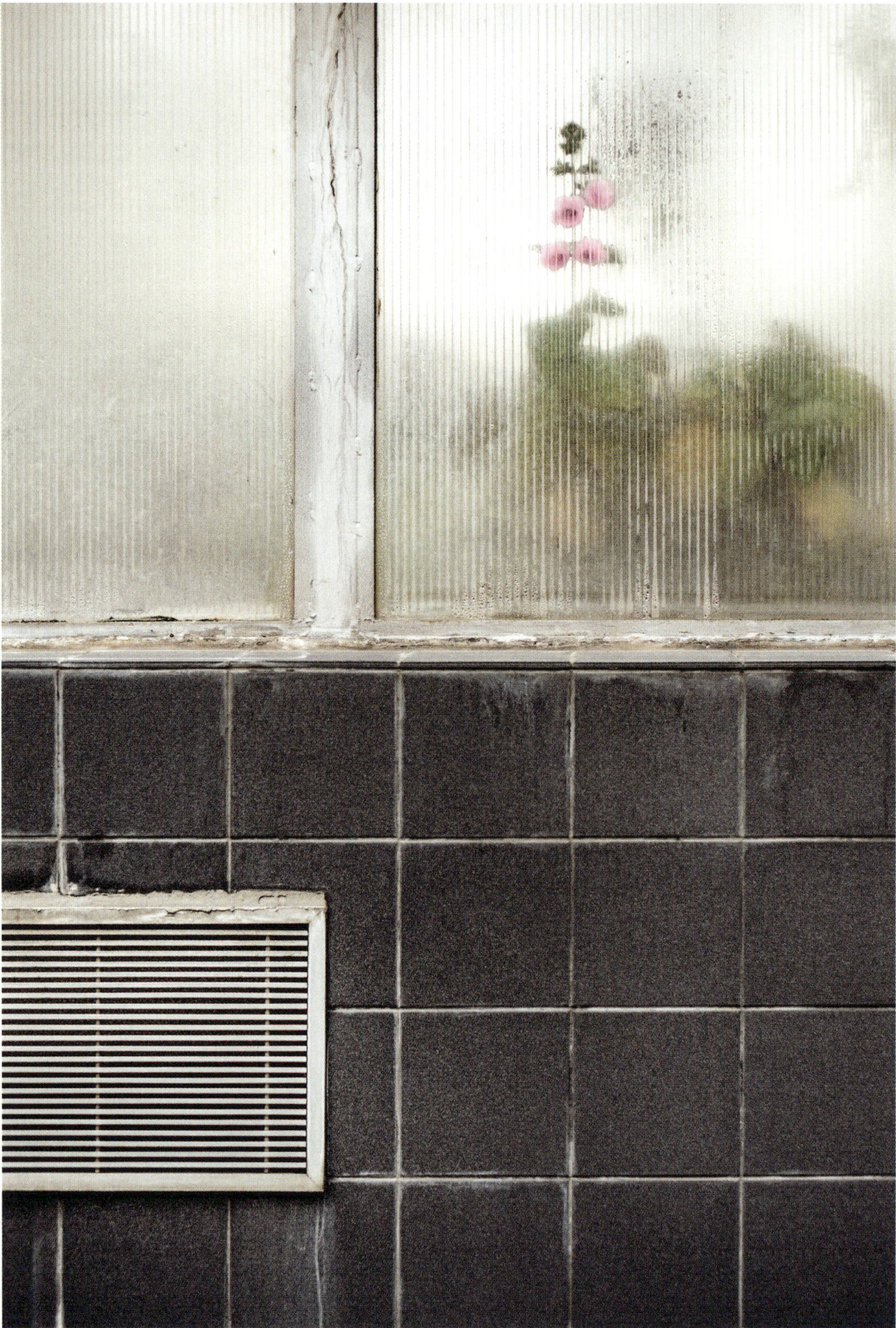

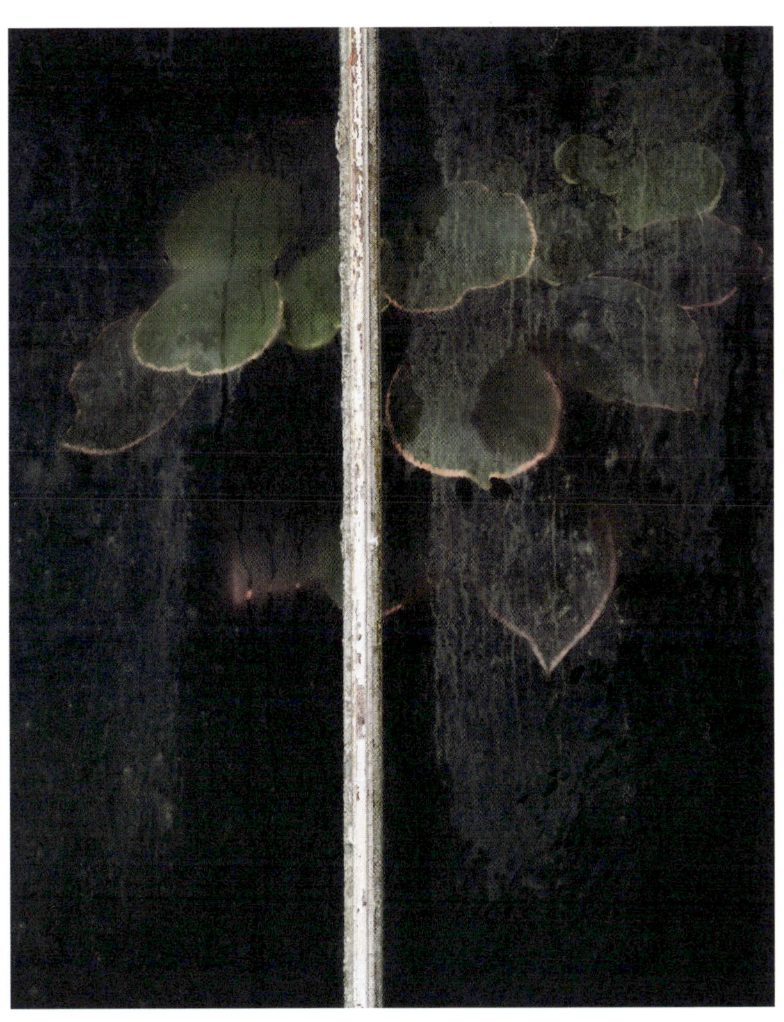

   Brno, Czech Republic *(opposite)* Brussels, Belgium *(above)*

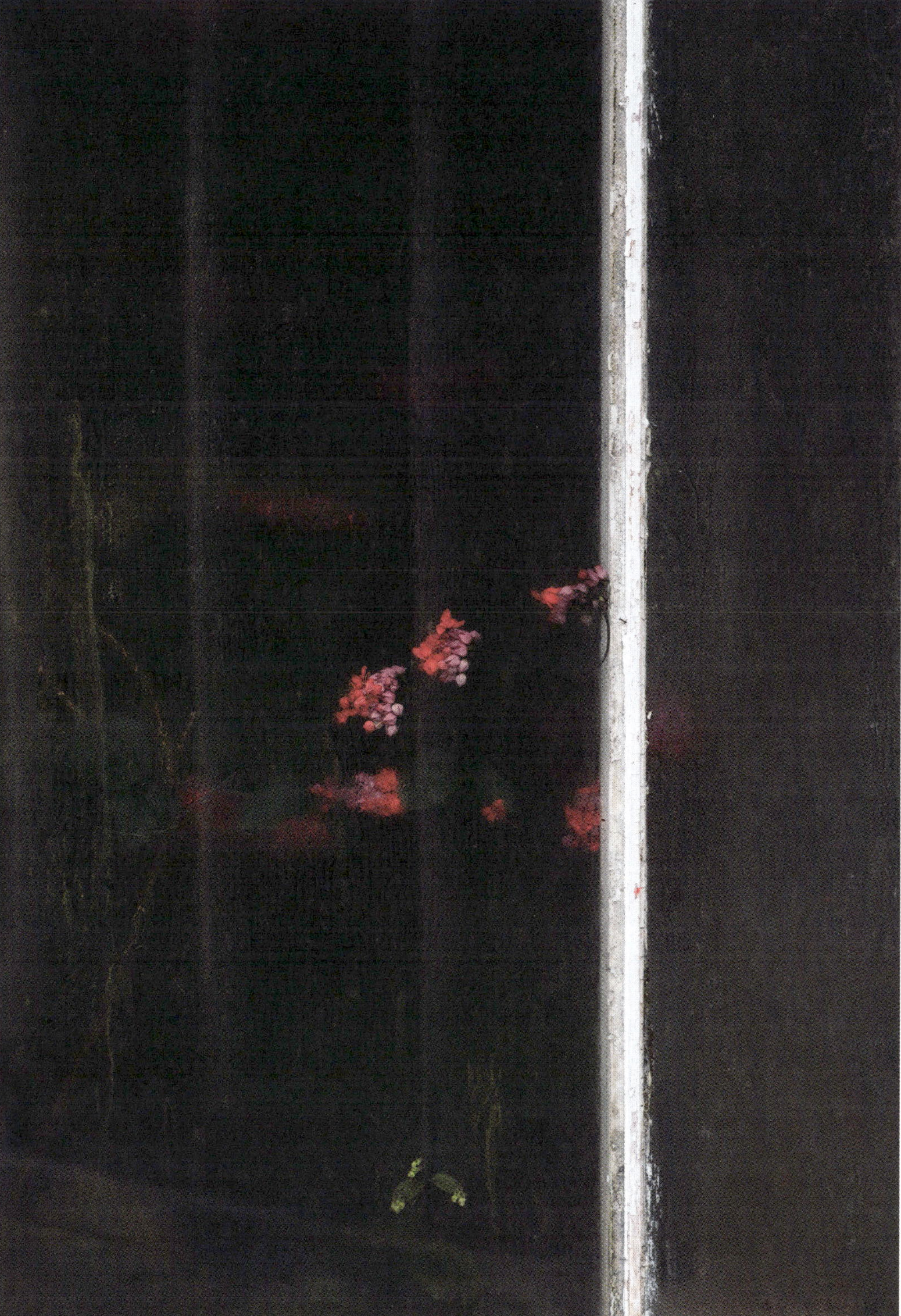

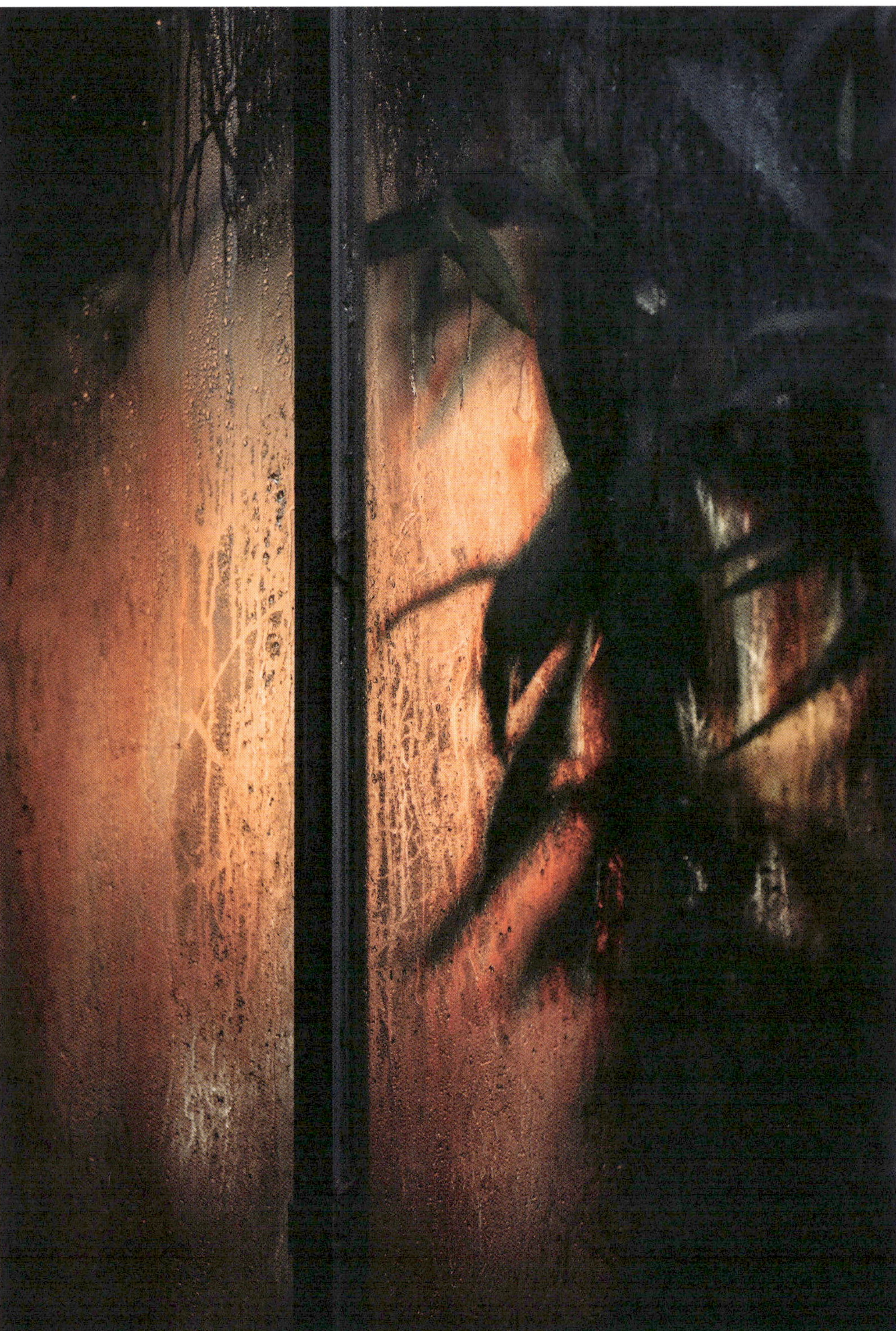

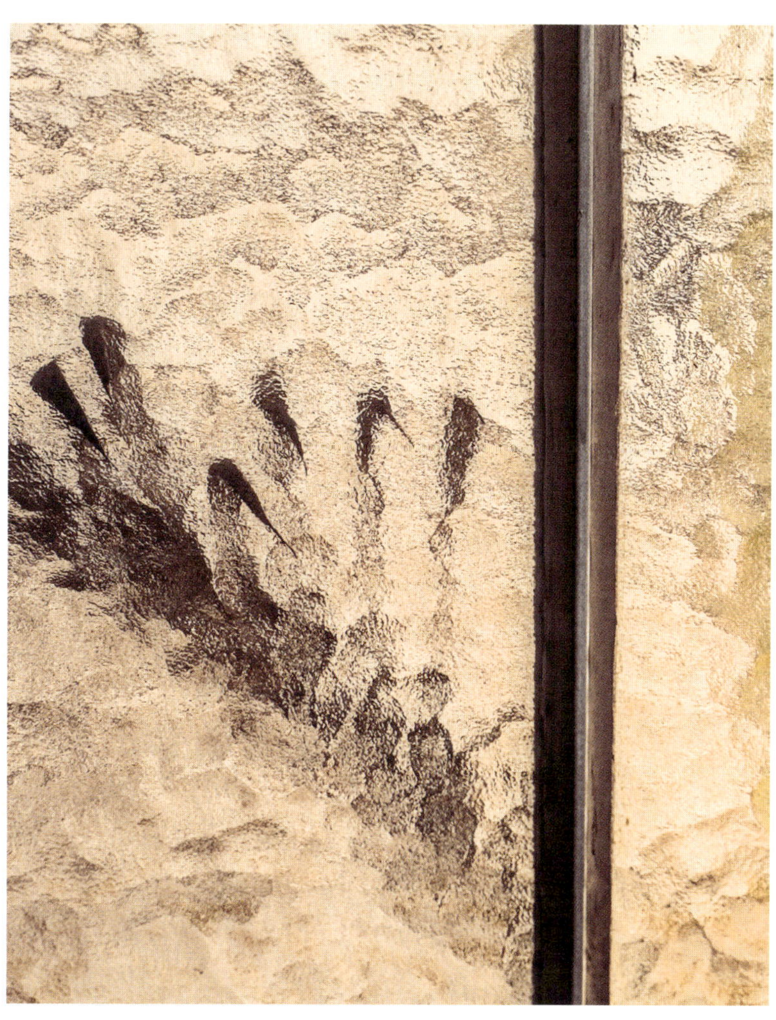

 Warsaw, Poland *(opposite)* Geneva, Switzerland *(above)*

Edinburgh, Scotland

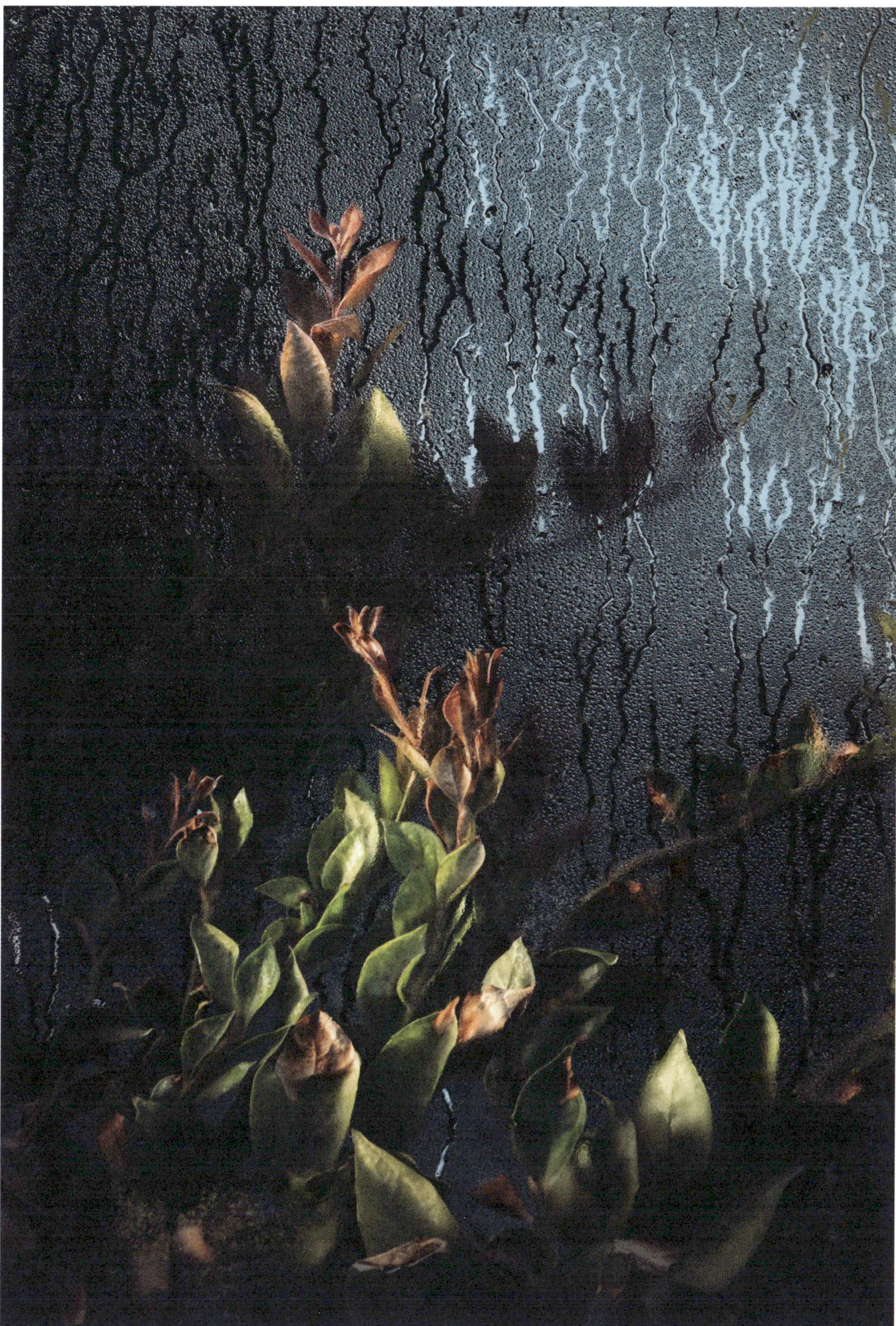

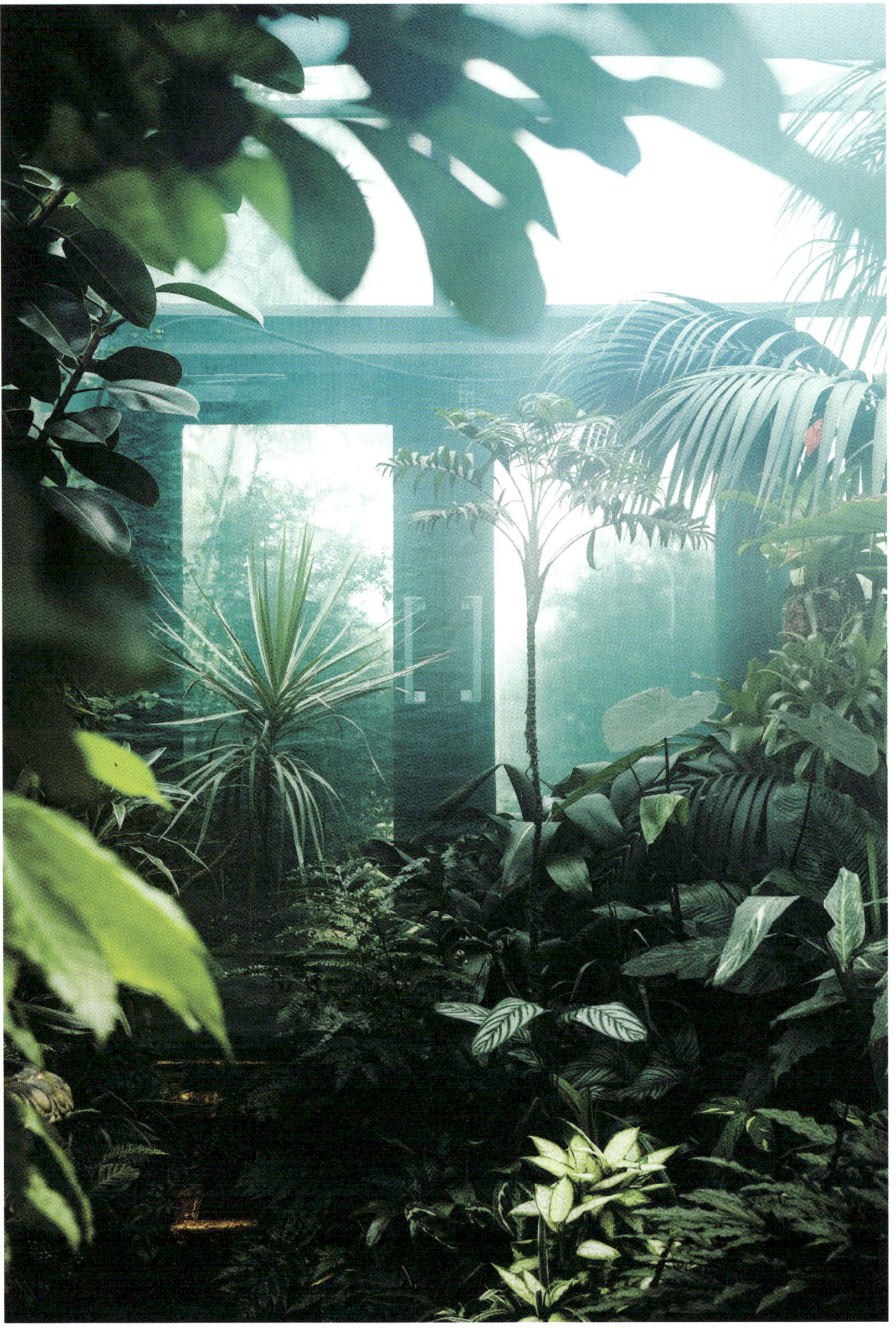

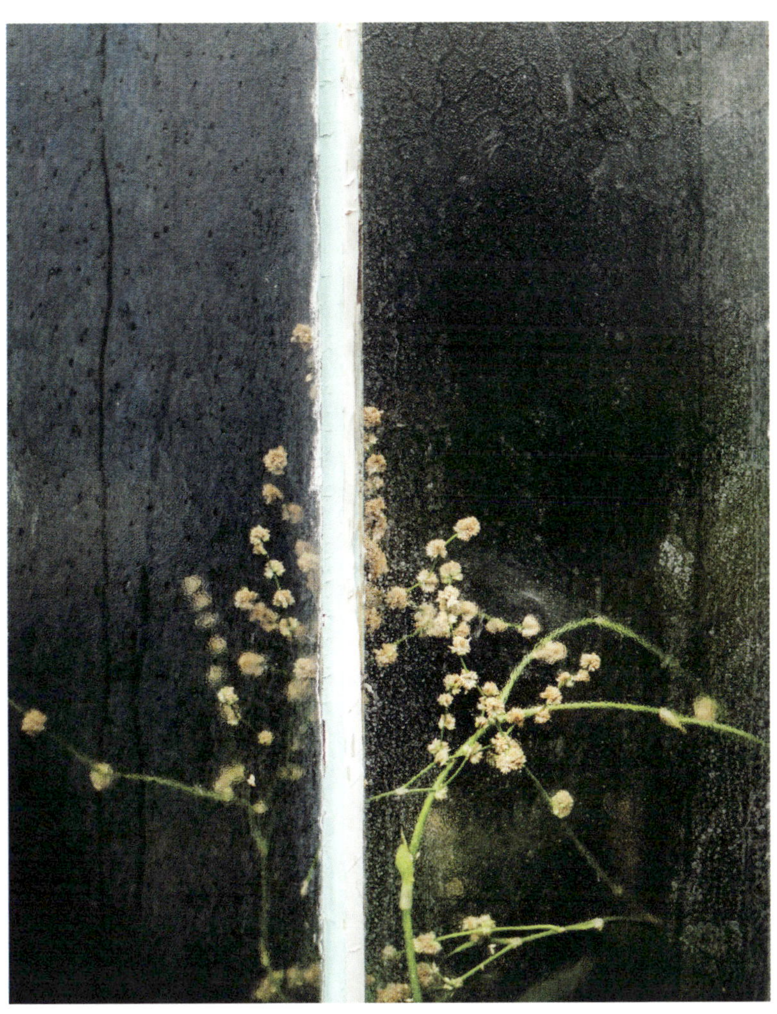

57   Aberdeen, Scotland *(opposite)* Paris, France *(above)*

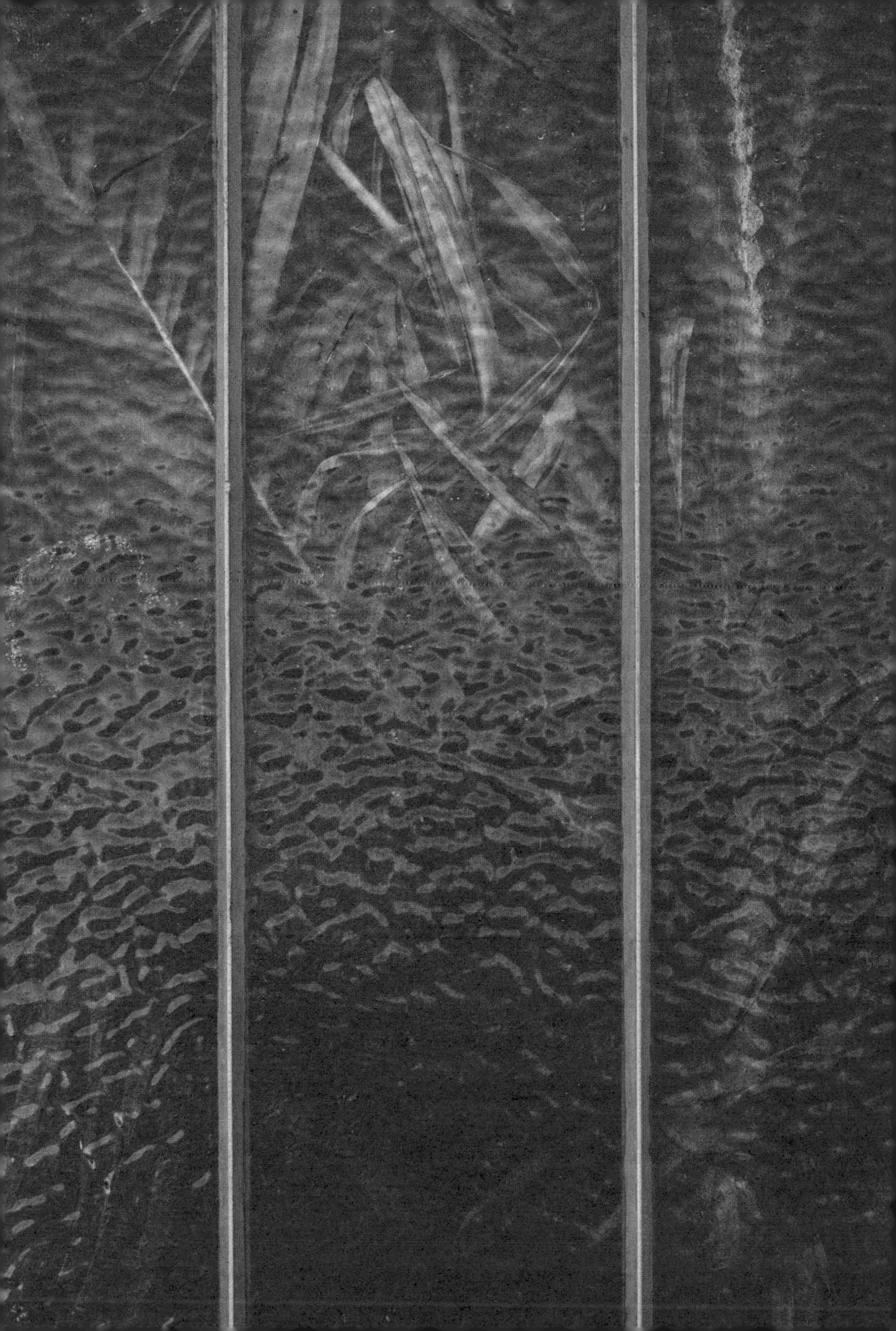

Geneva, Switzerland *(opposite)* Glasgow, Scotland *(overleaf)*

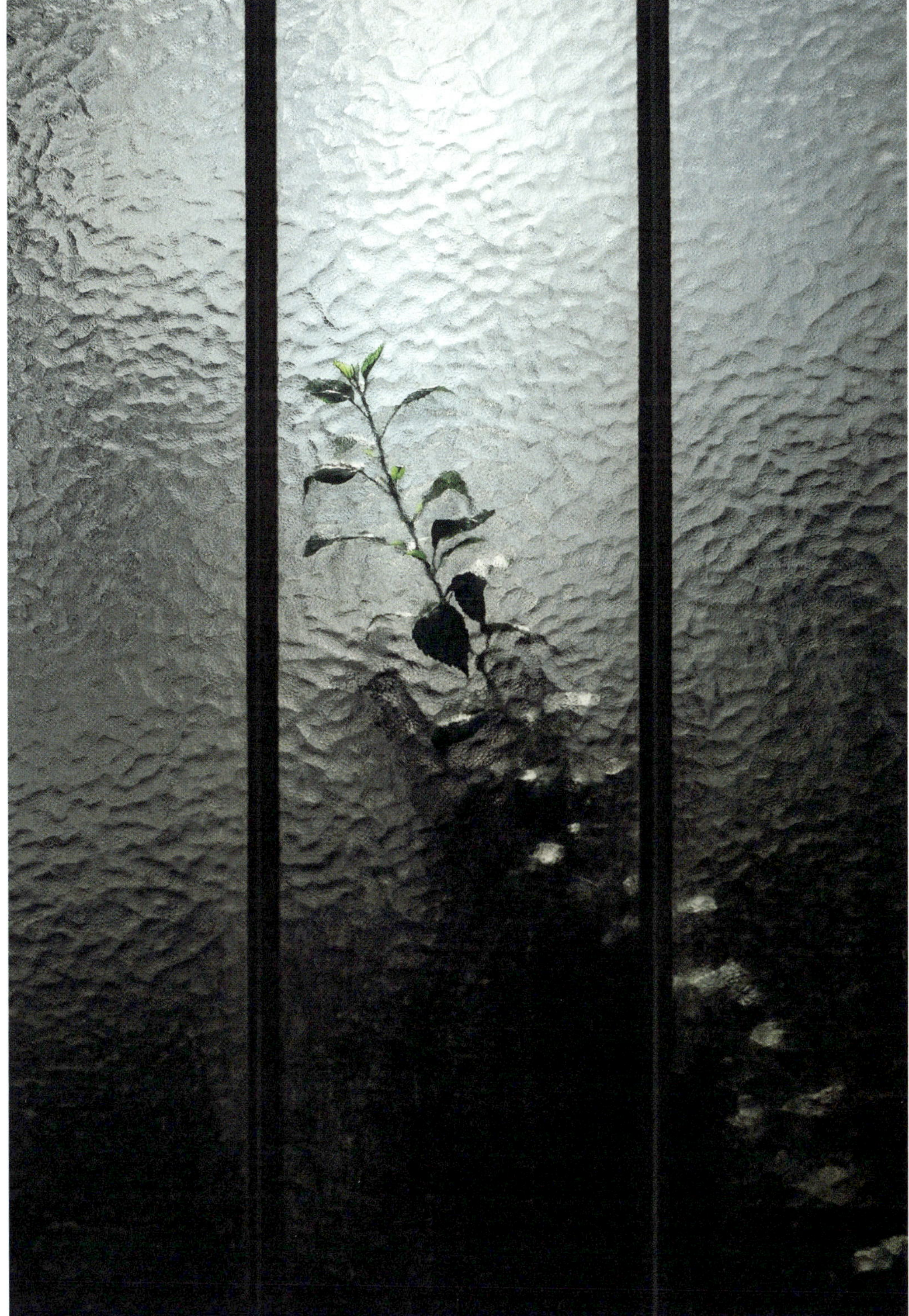

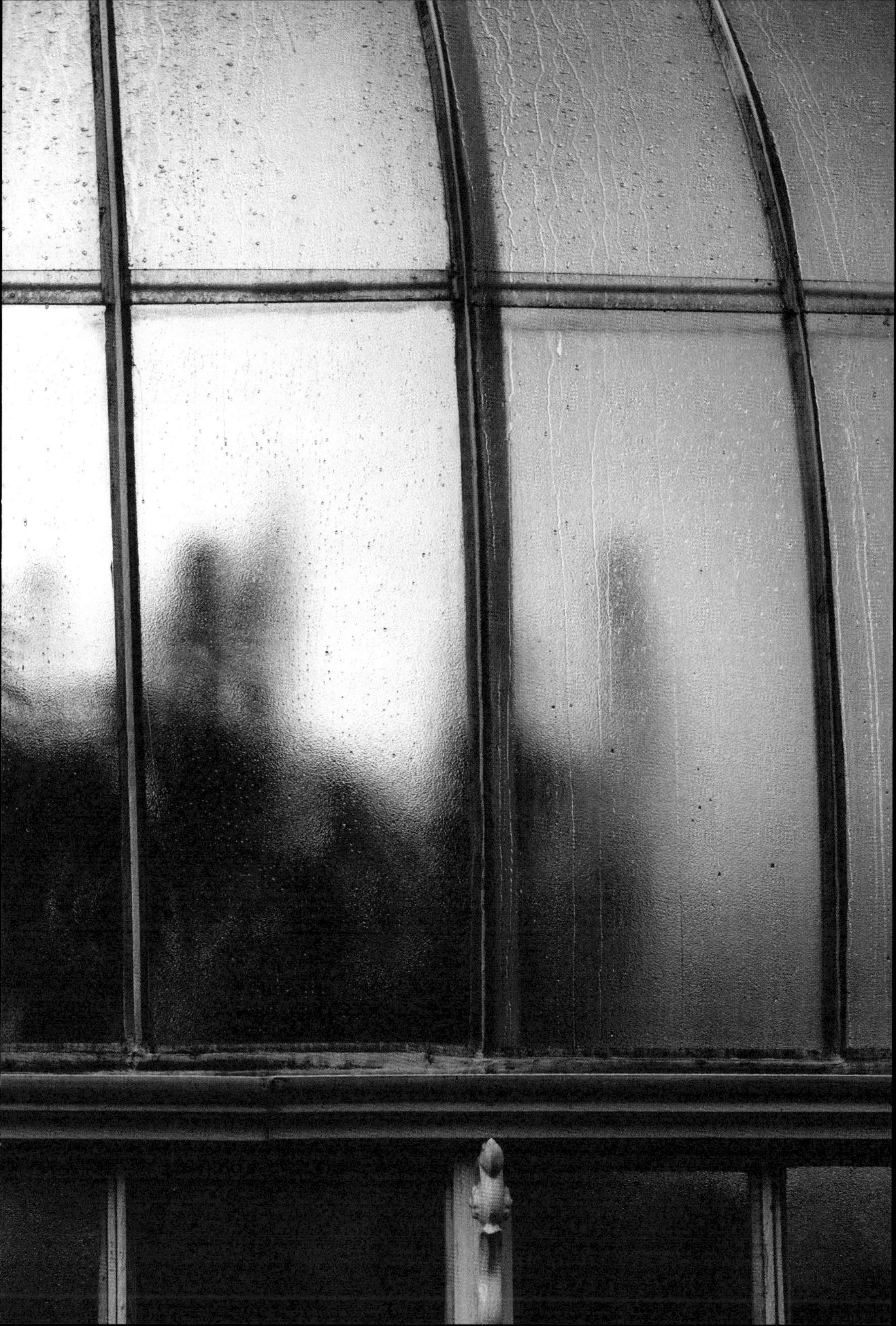

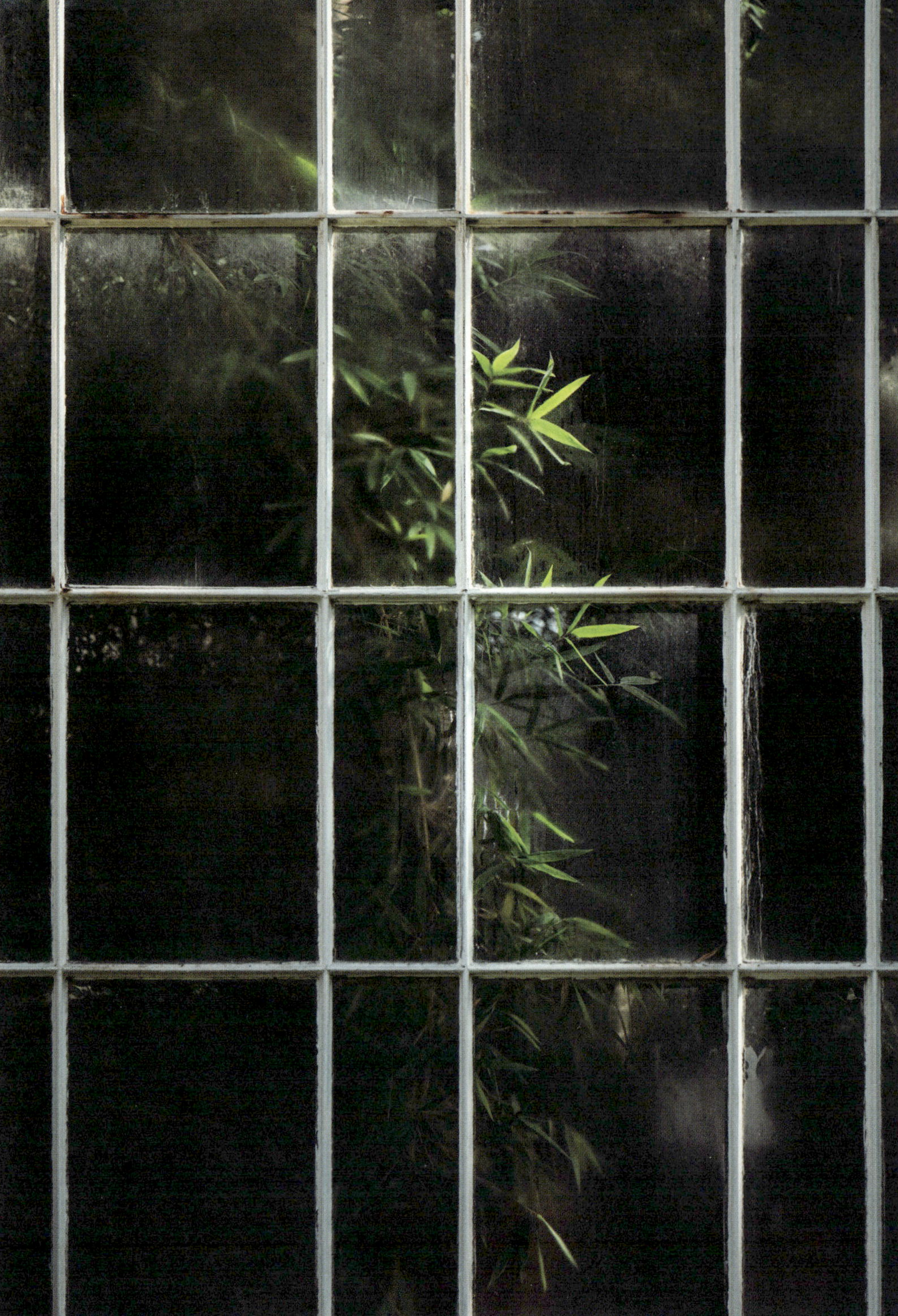

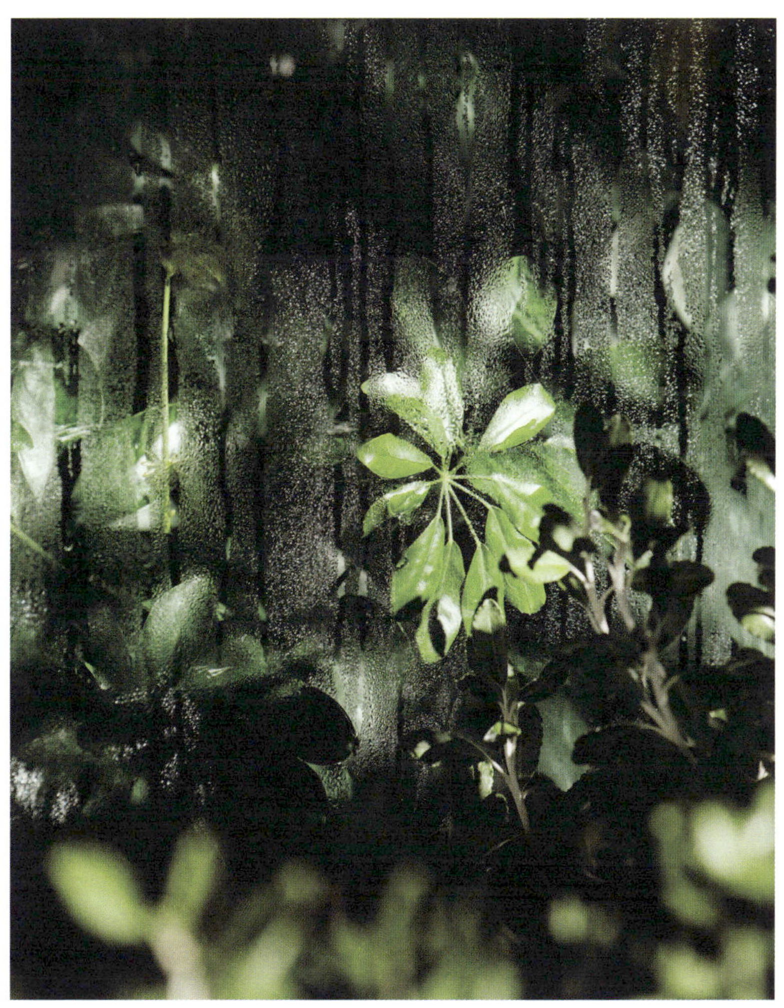

    Edinburgh, Scotland

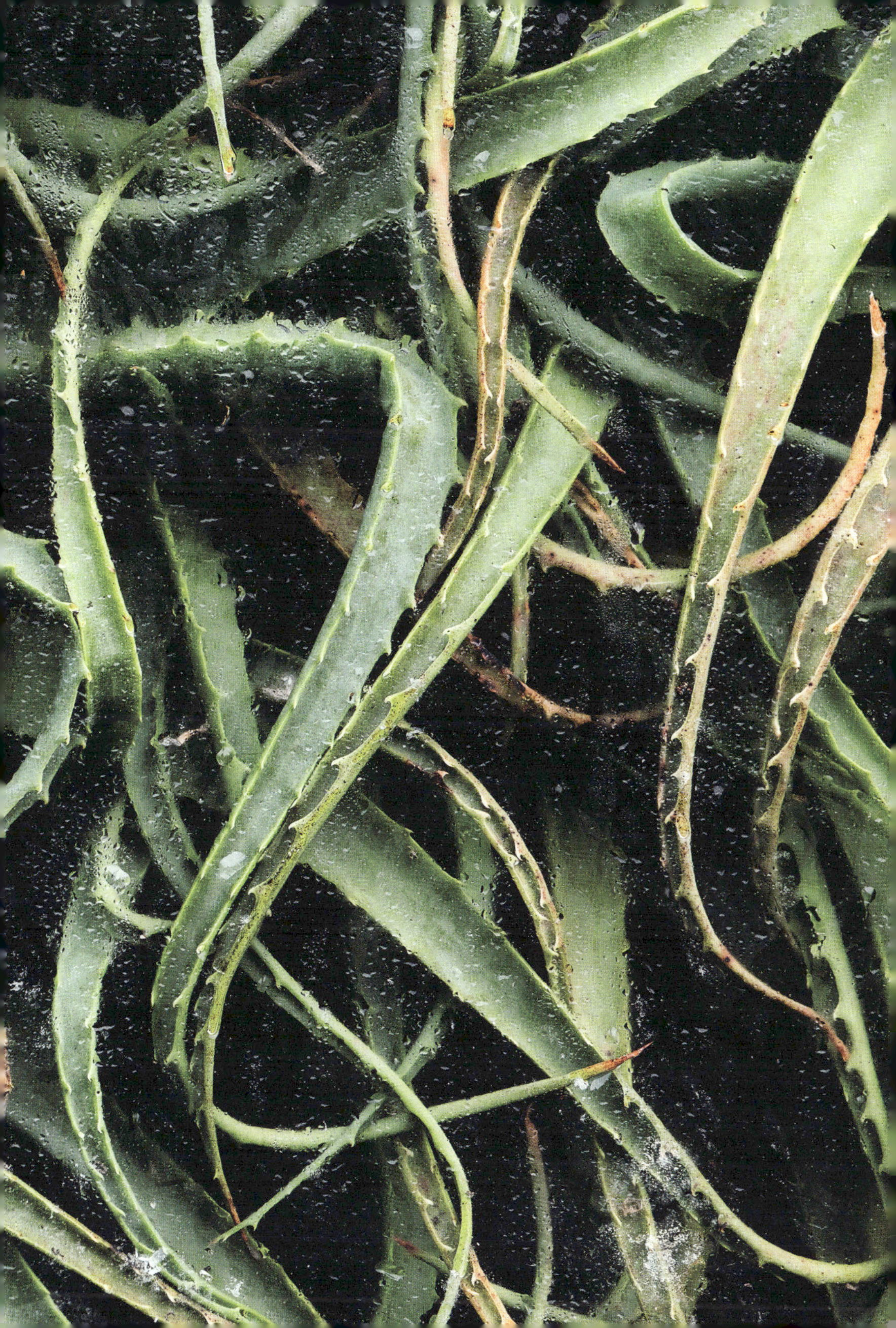

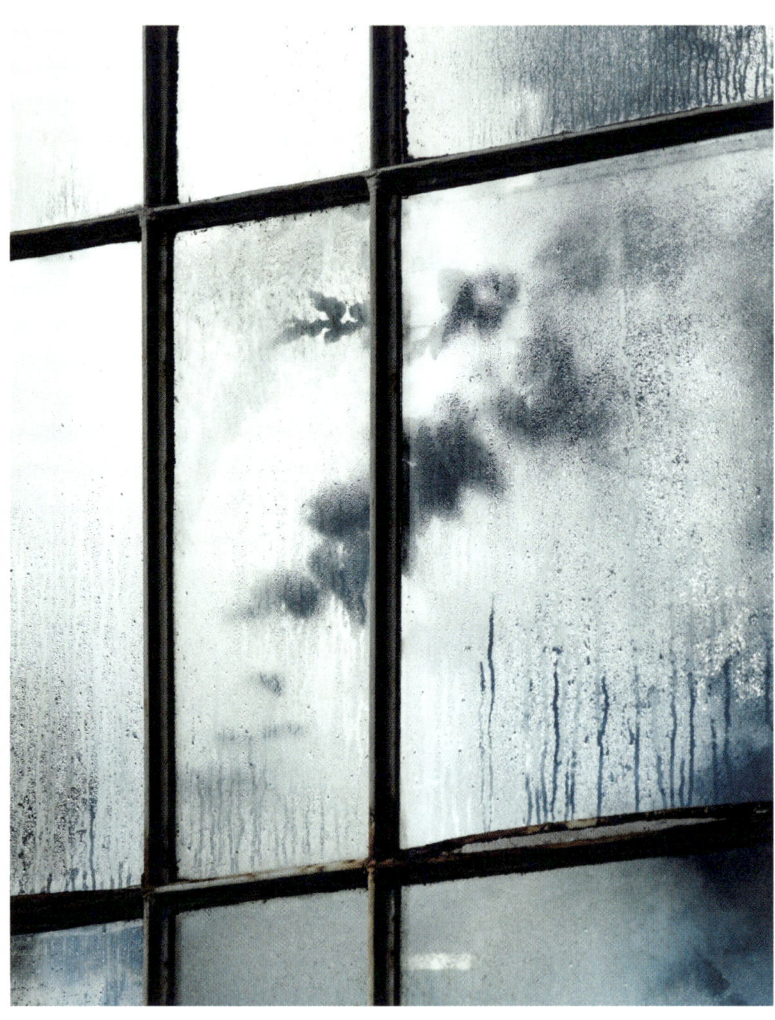

     Edinburgh, Scotland *(above)* Dundee, Scotland *(opposite)*

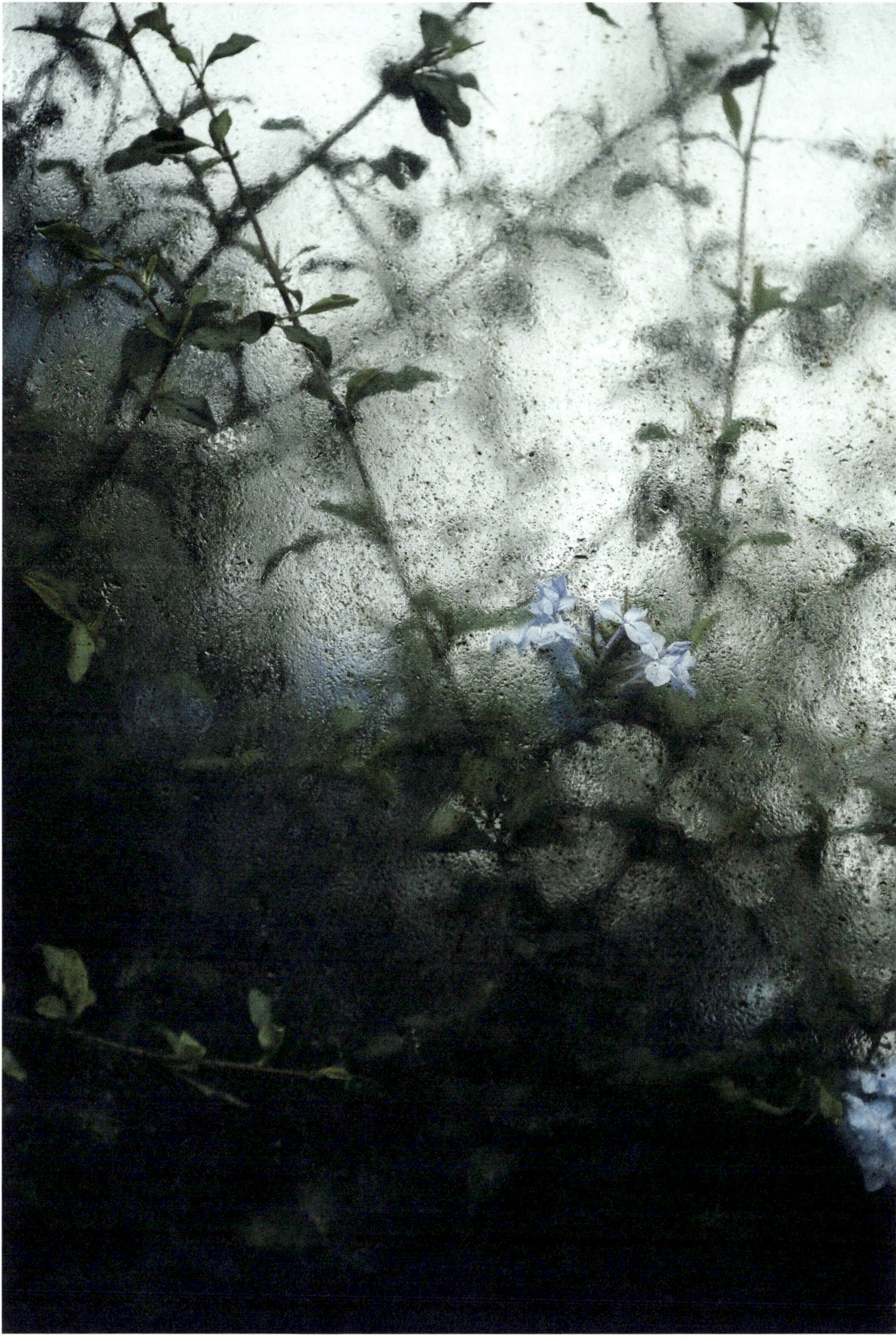

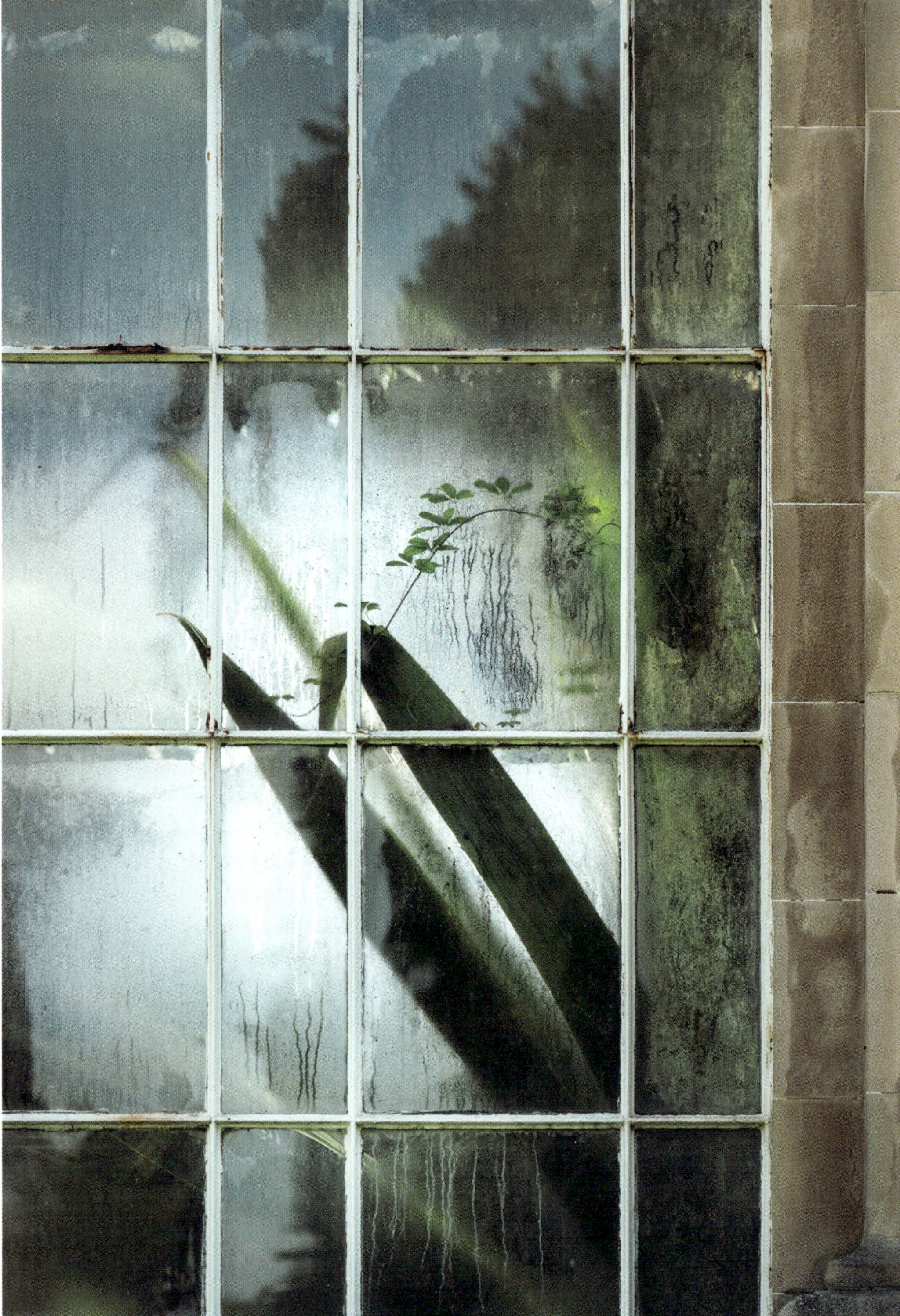

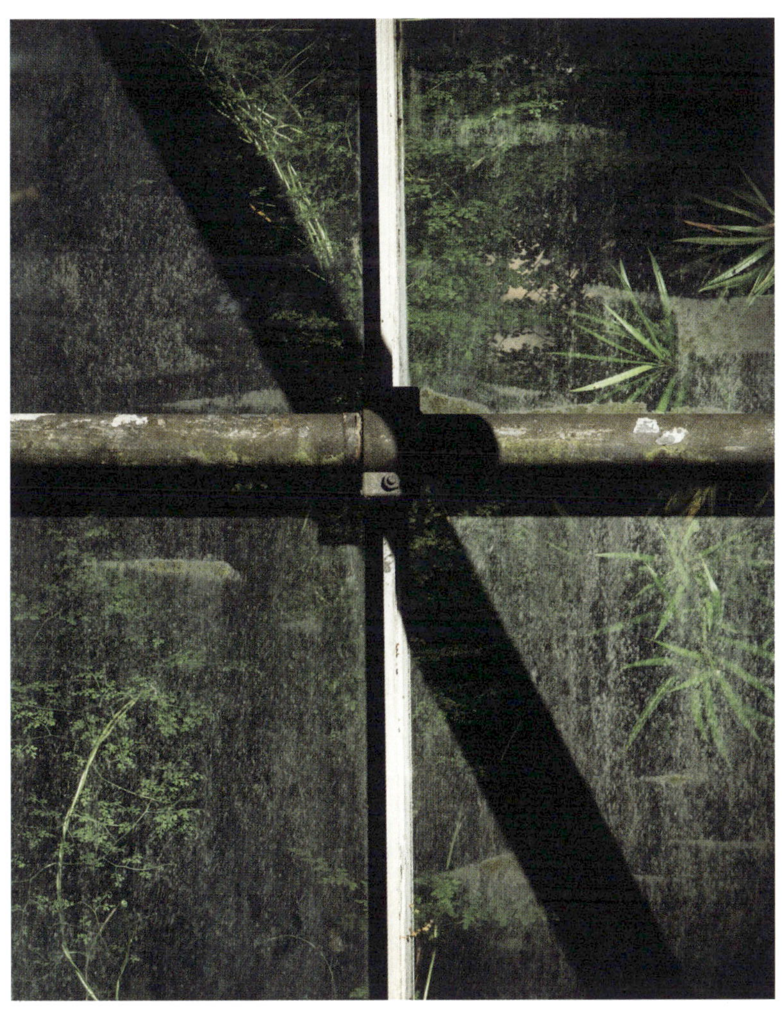

71   Edinburgh, Scotland

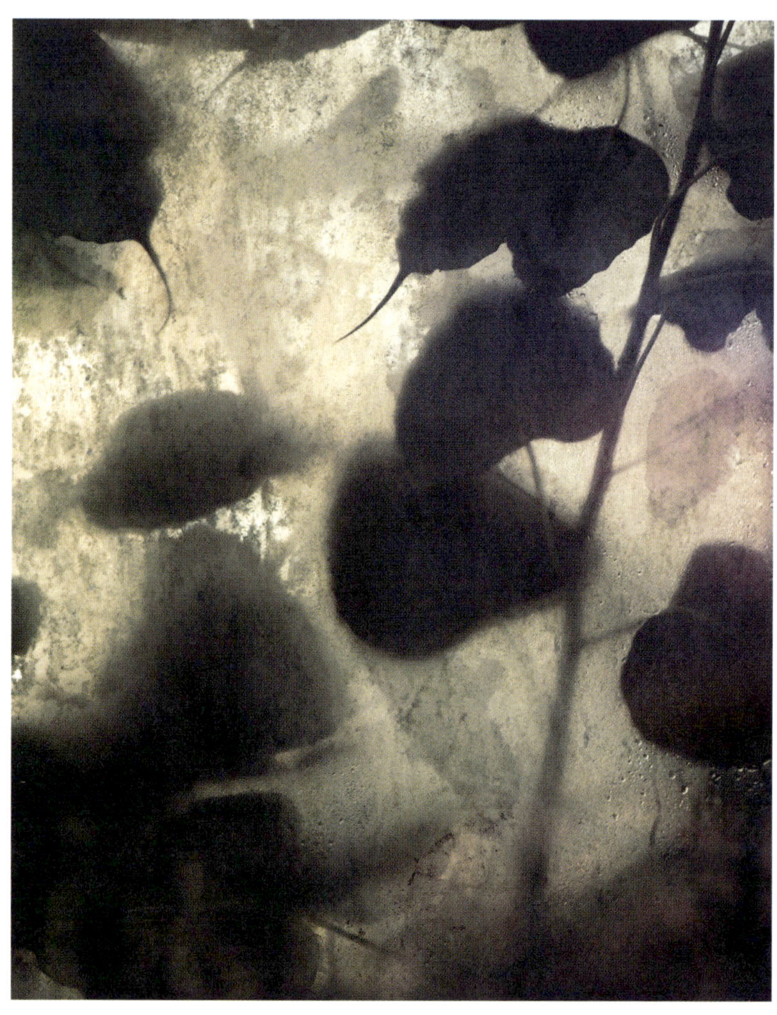

72   Liège, Belgium (*above & opposite*) Kraków, Poland (*overleaf*)

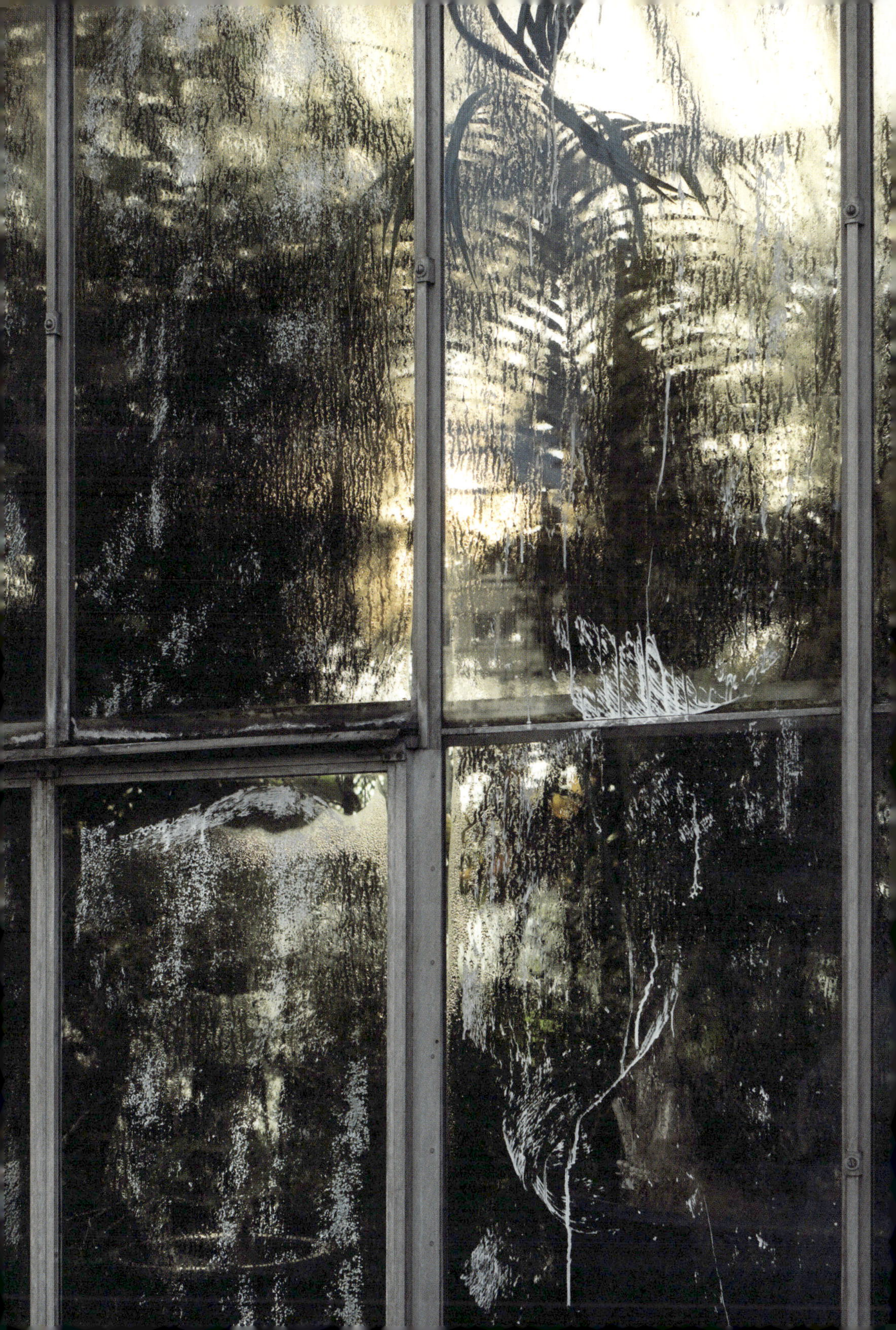

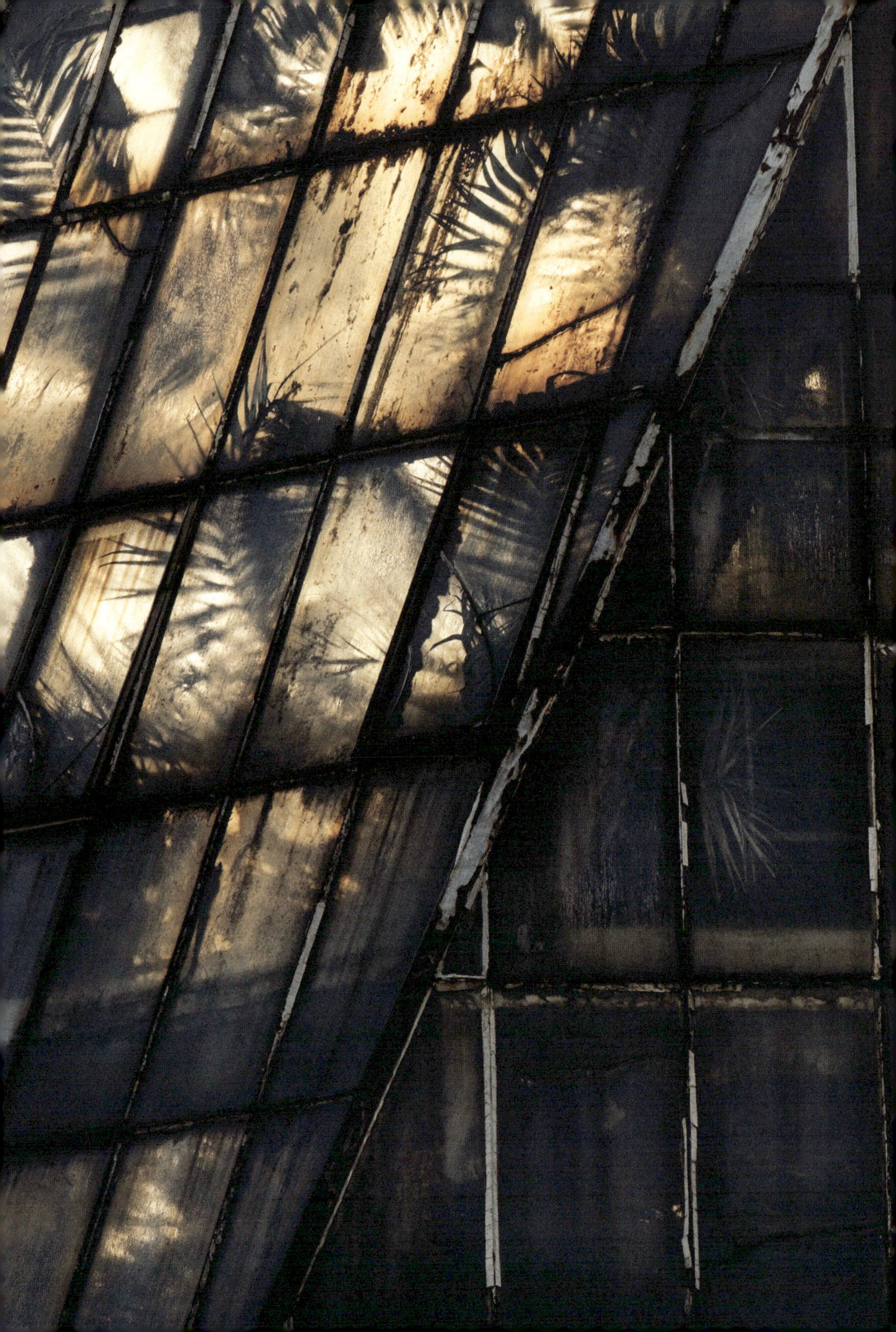

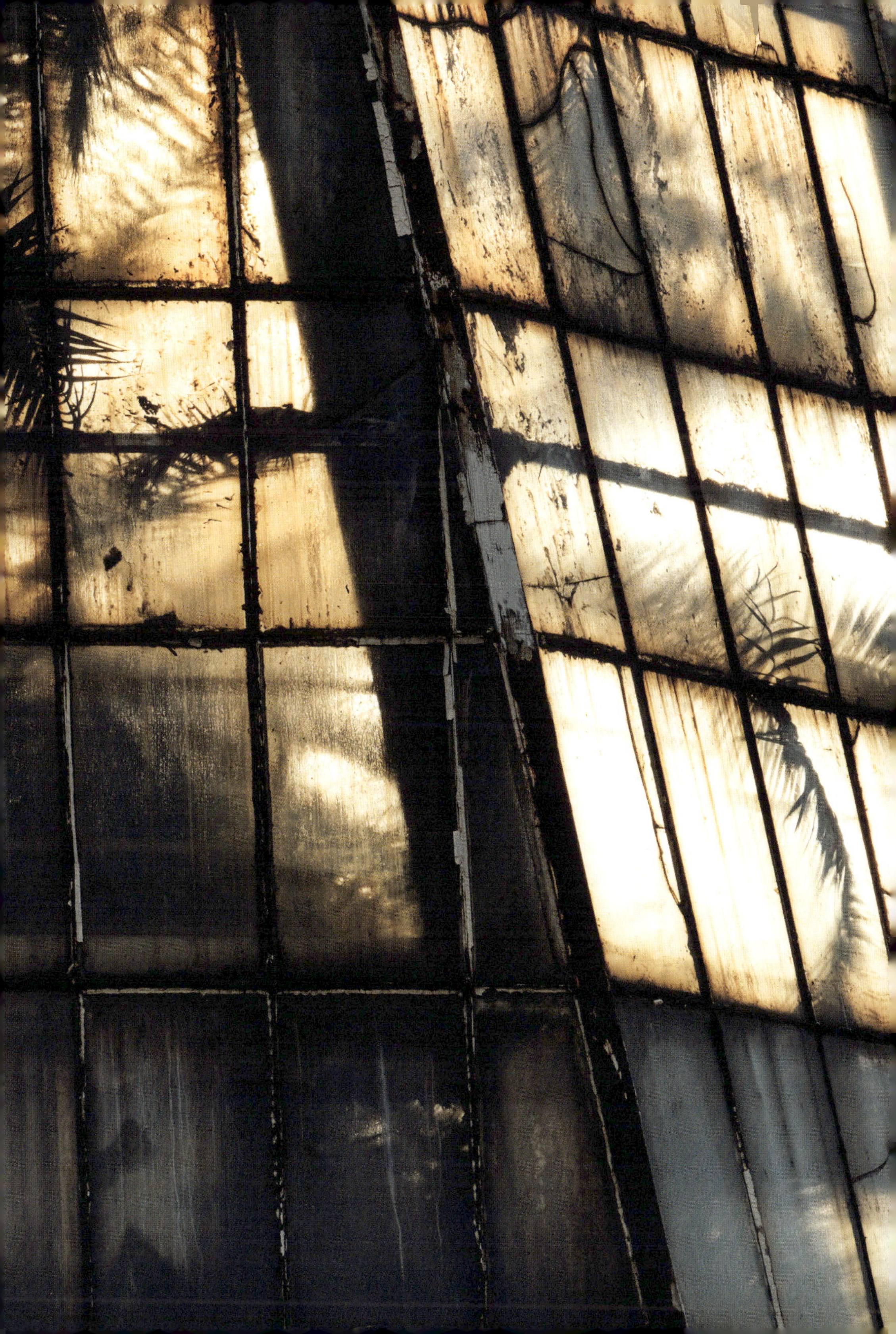

     Warsaw, Poland *(opposite)* Paris, France *(overleaf)*

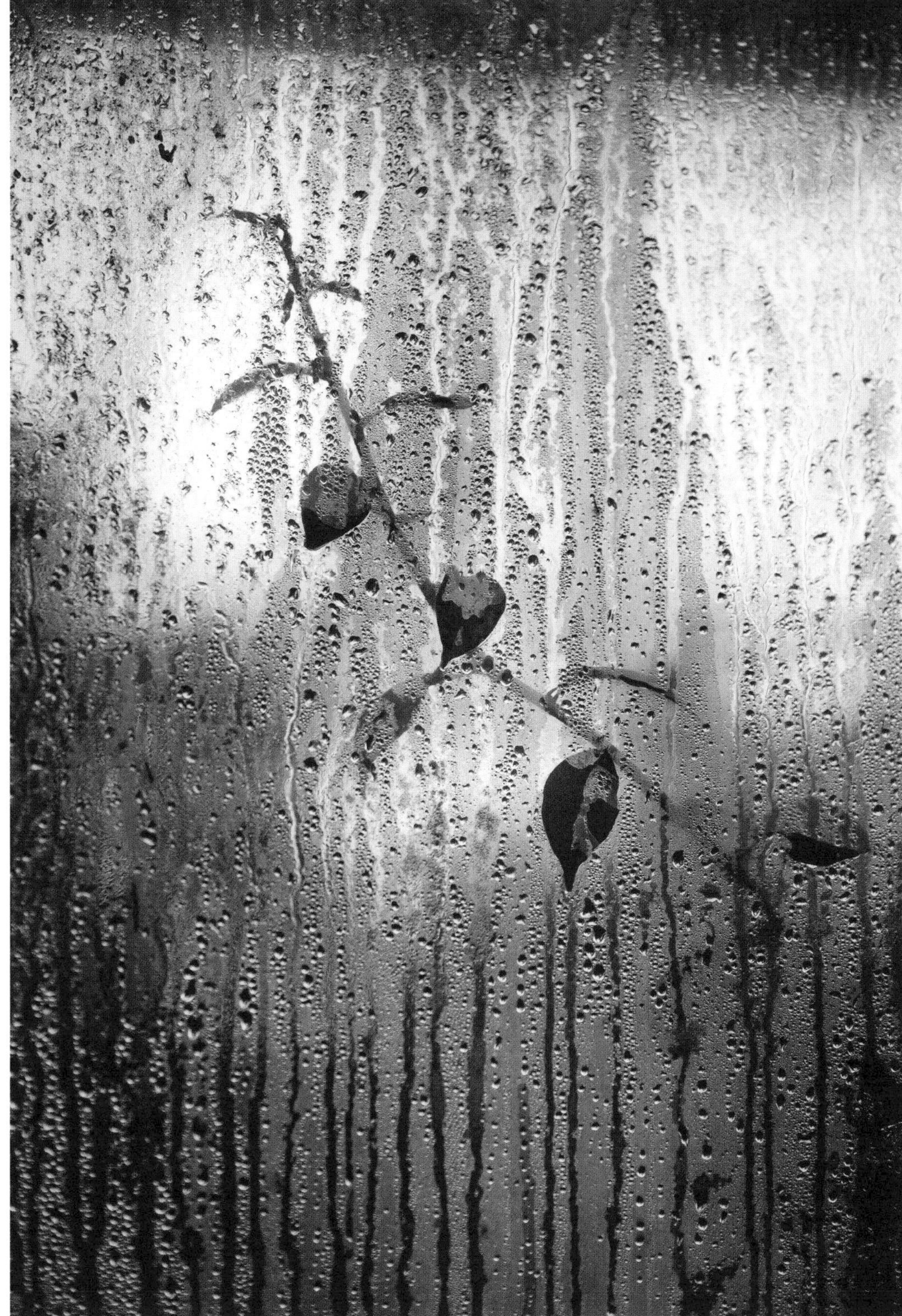

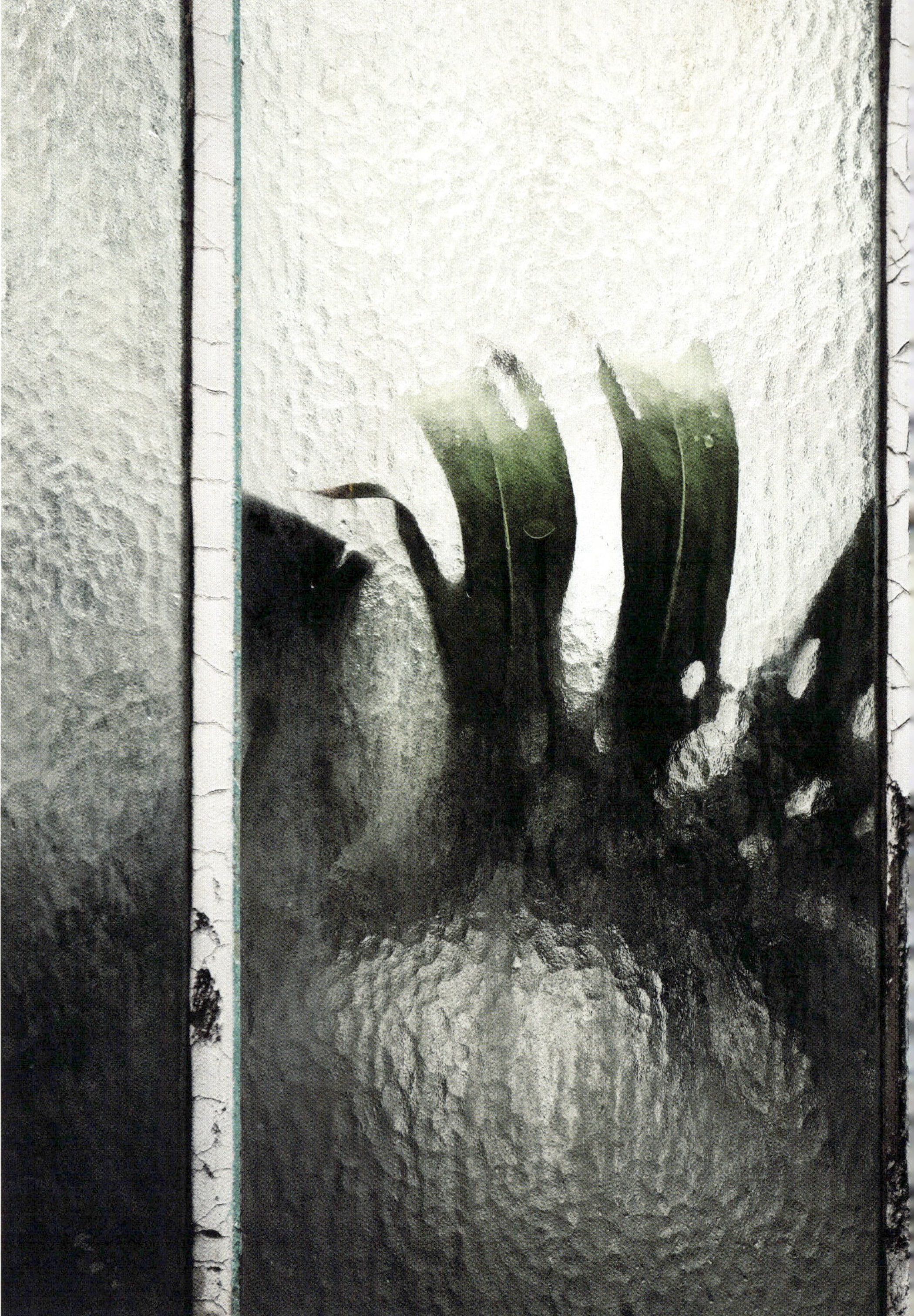

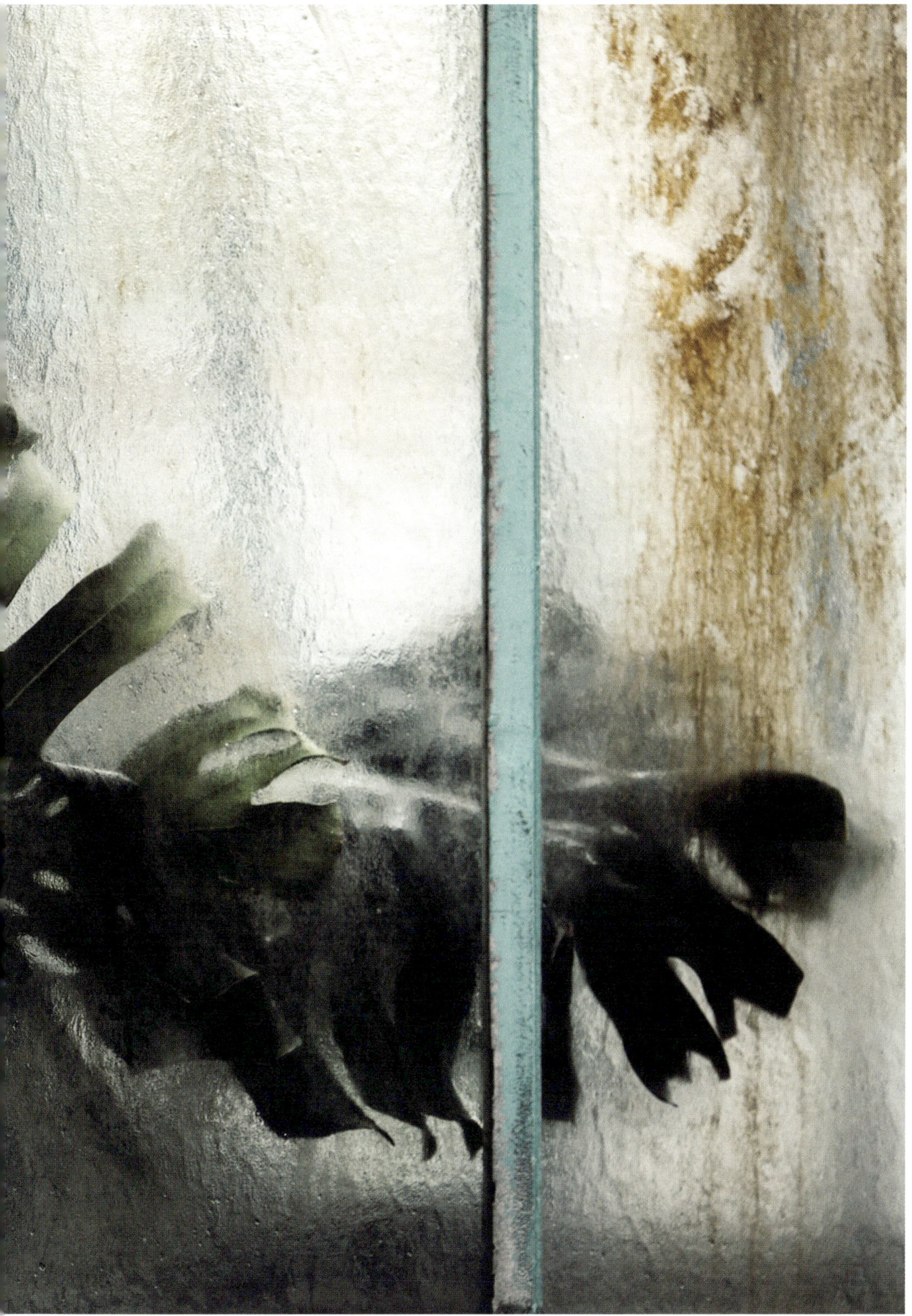

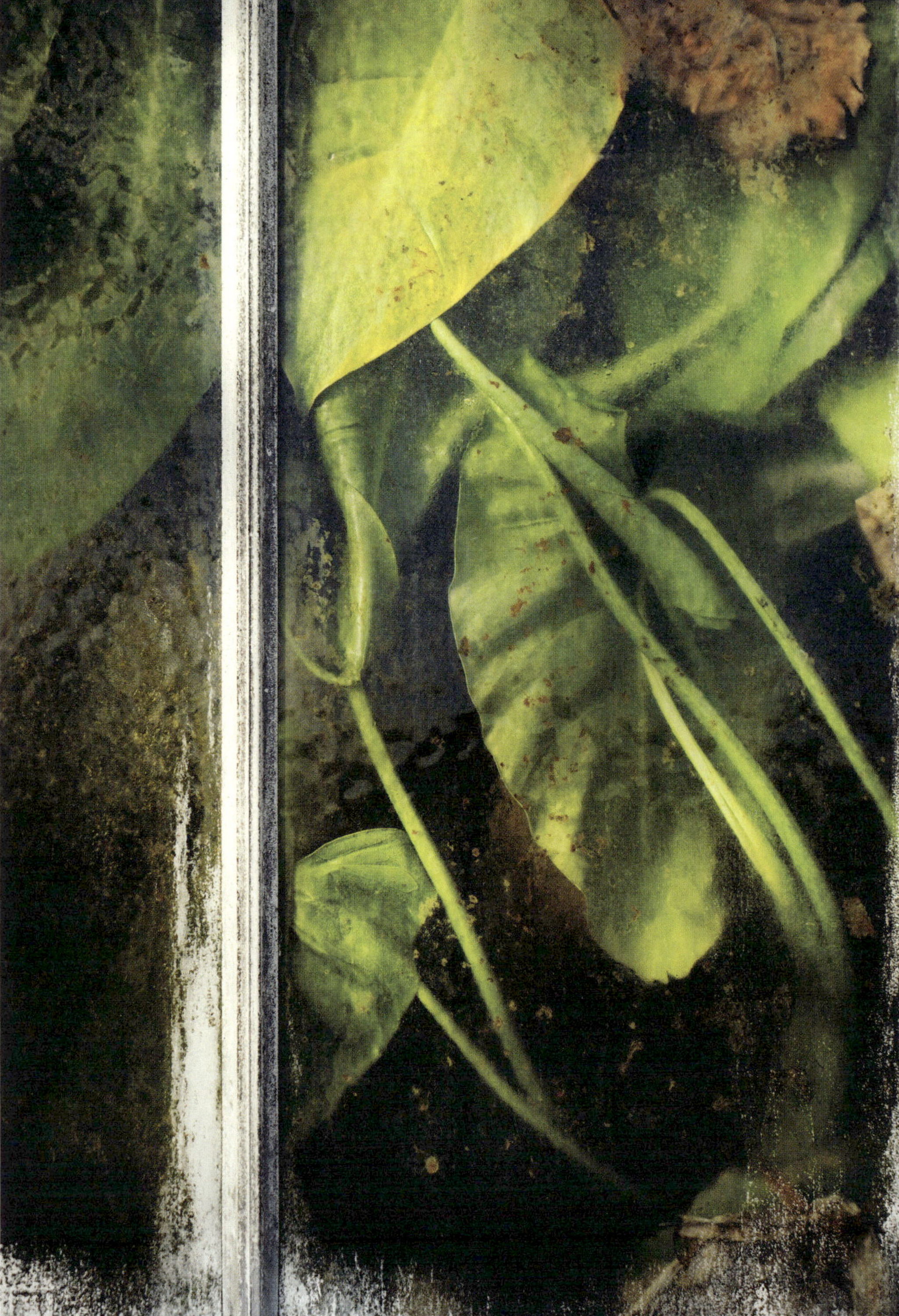

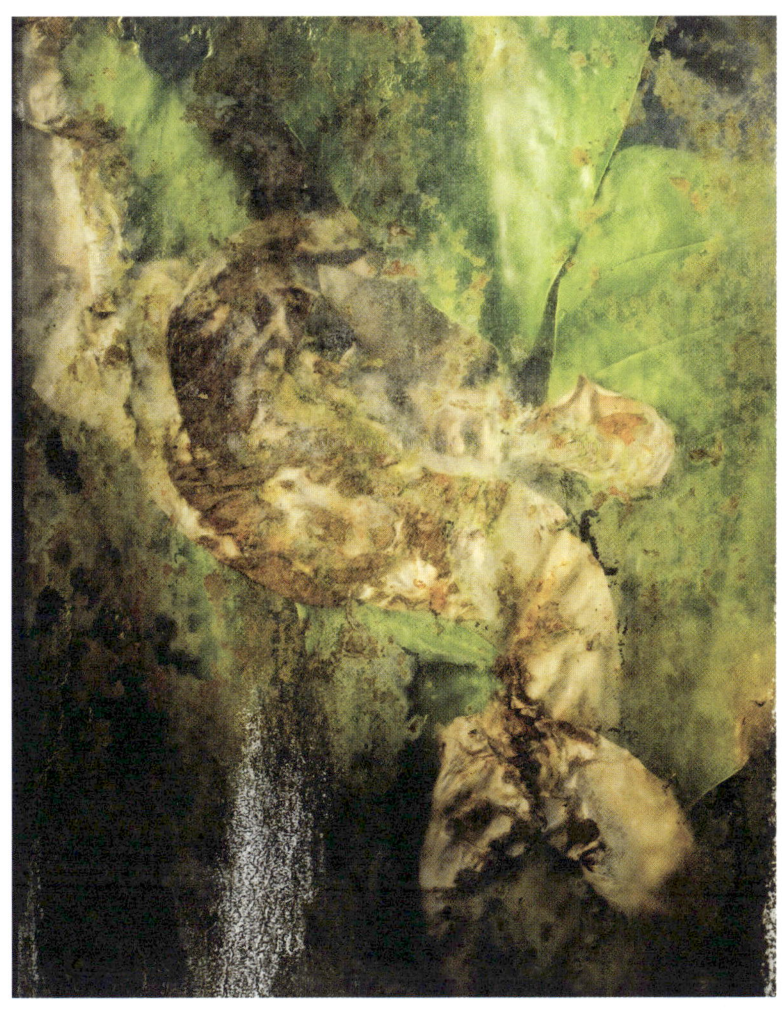

81   Ghent, Belgium

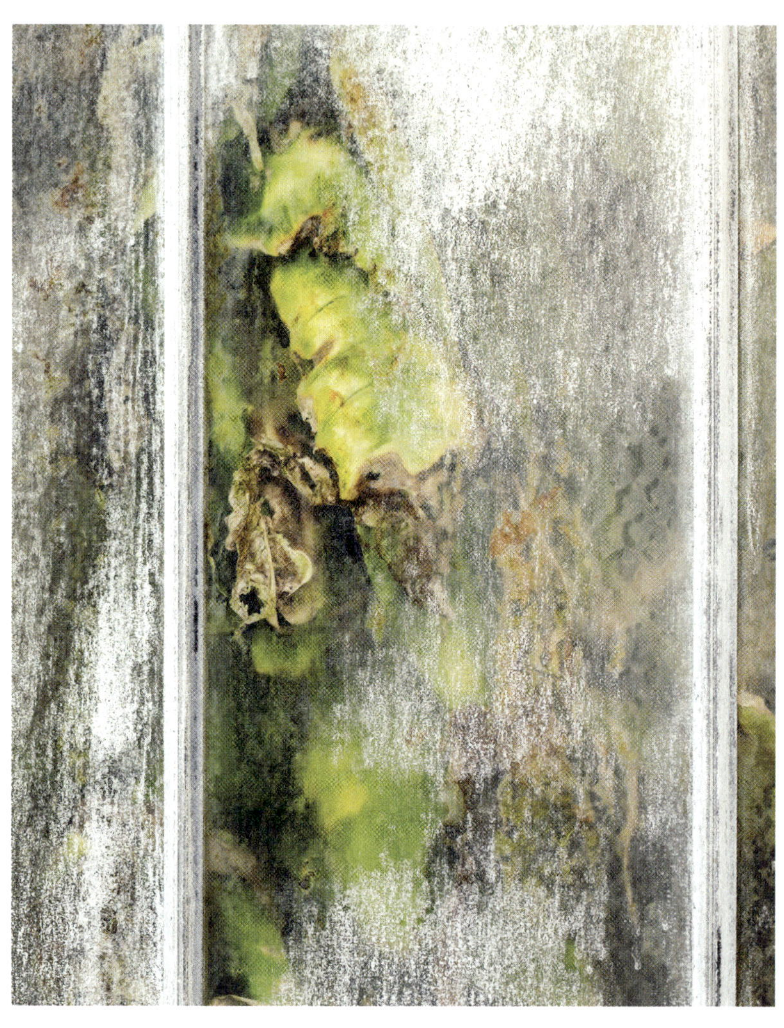

Ghent, Belgium *(above)* Paris, France *(opposite)*
Poznań, Poland *(overleaf)*

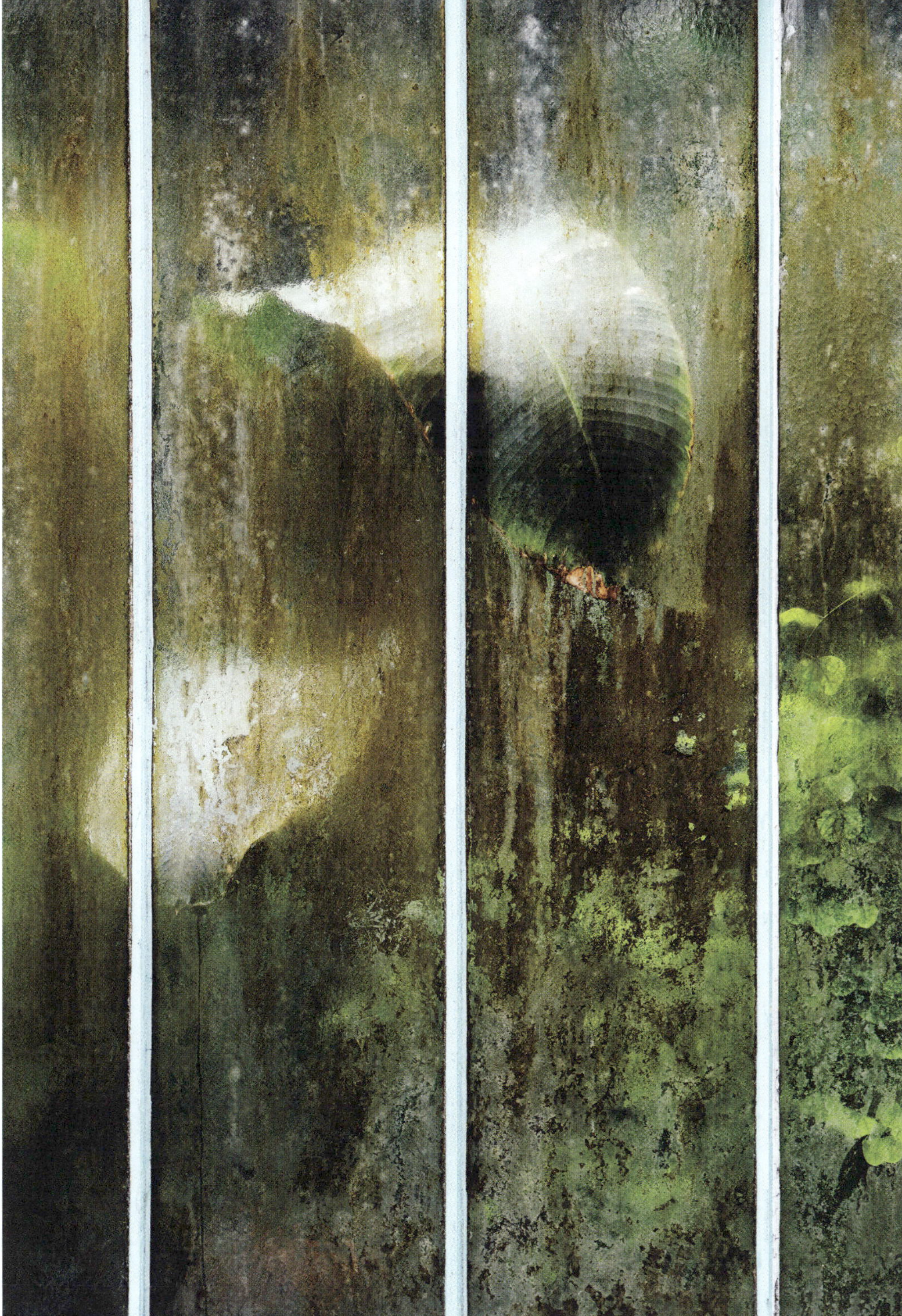

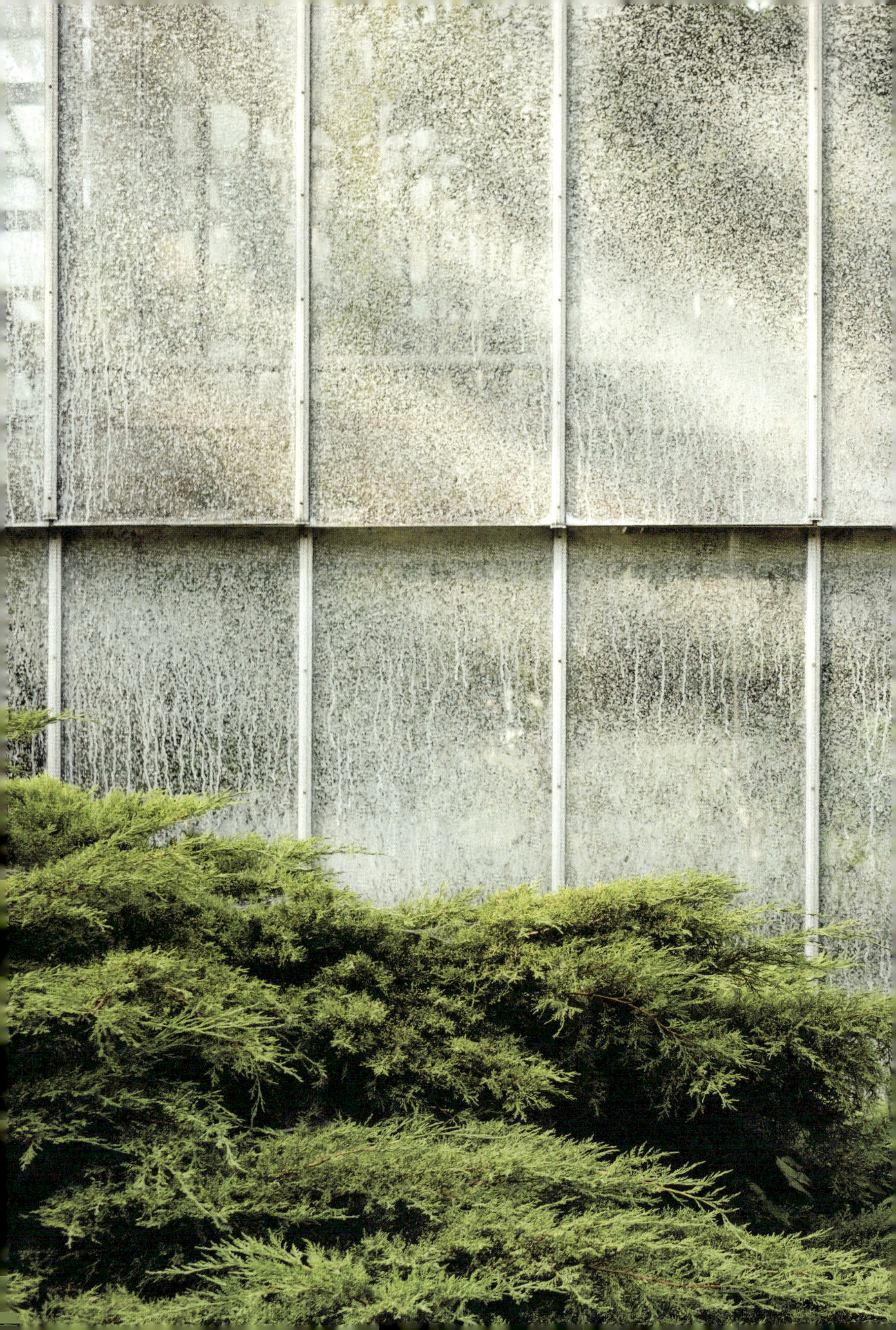

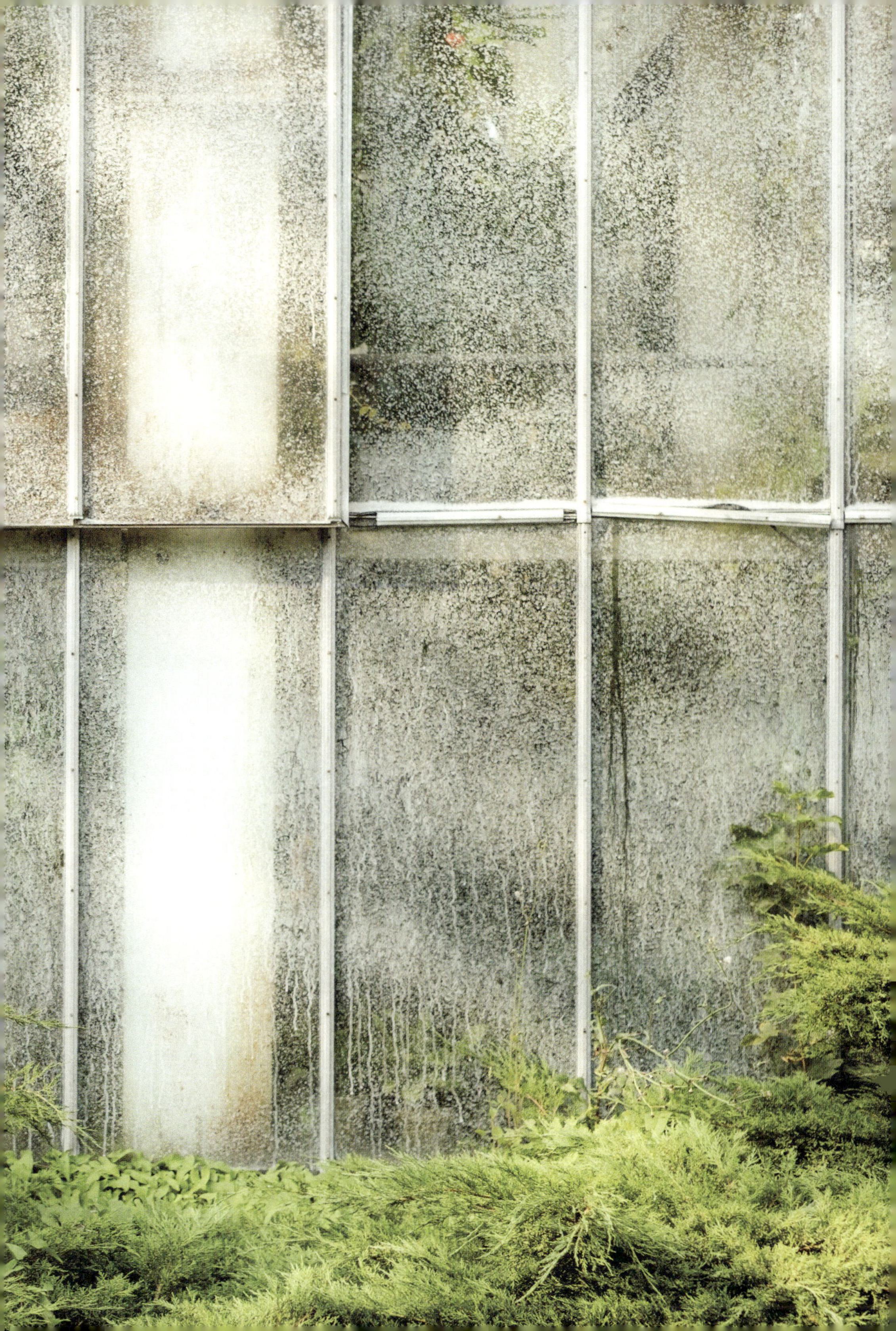

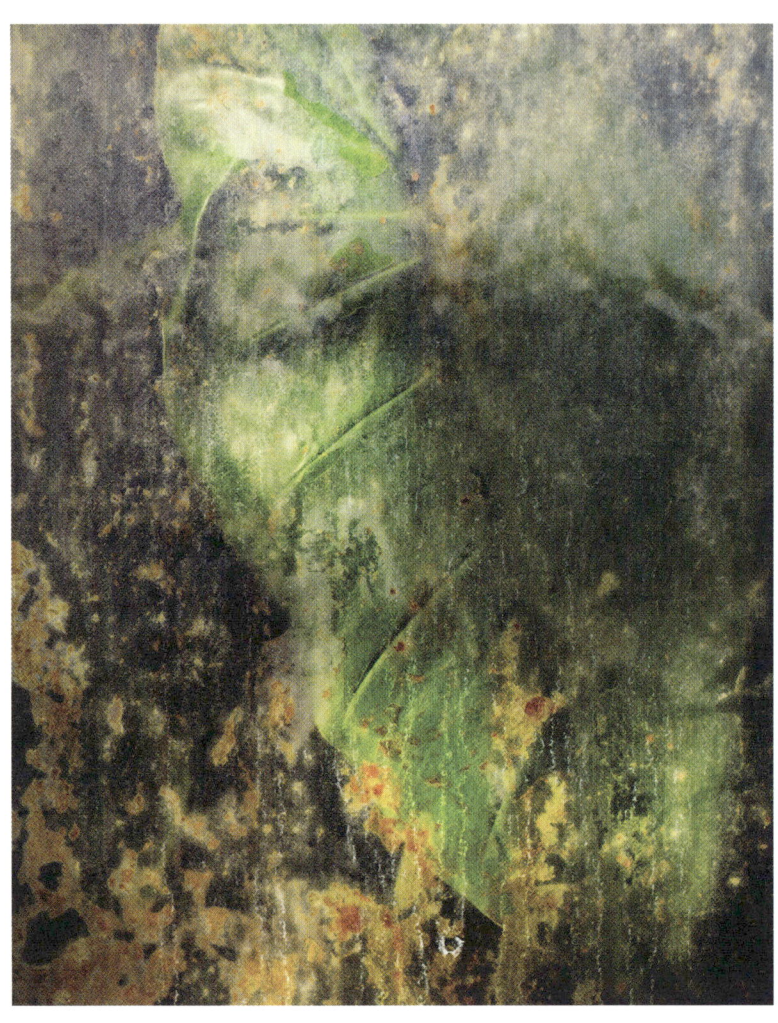

Ghent, Belgium *(above)* Nantes, France *(opposite)*

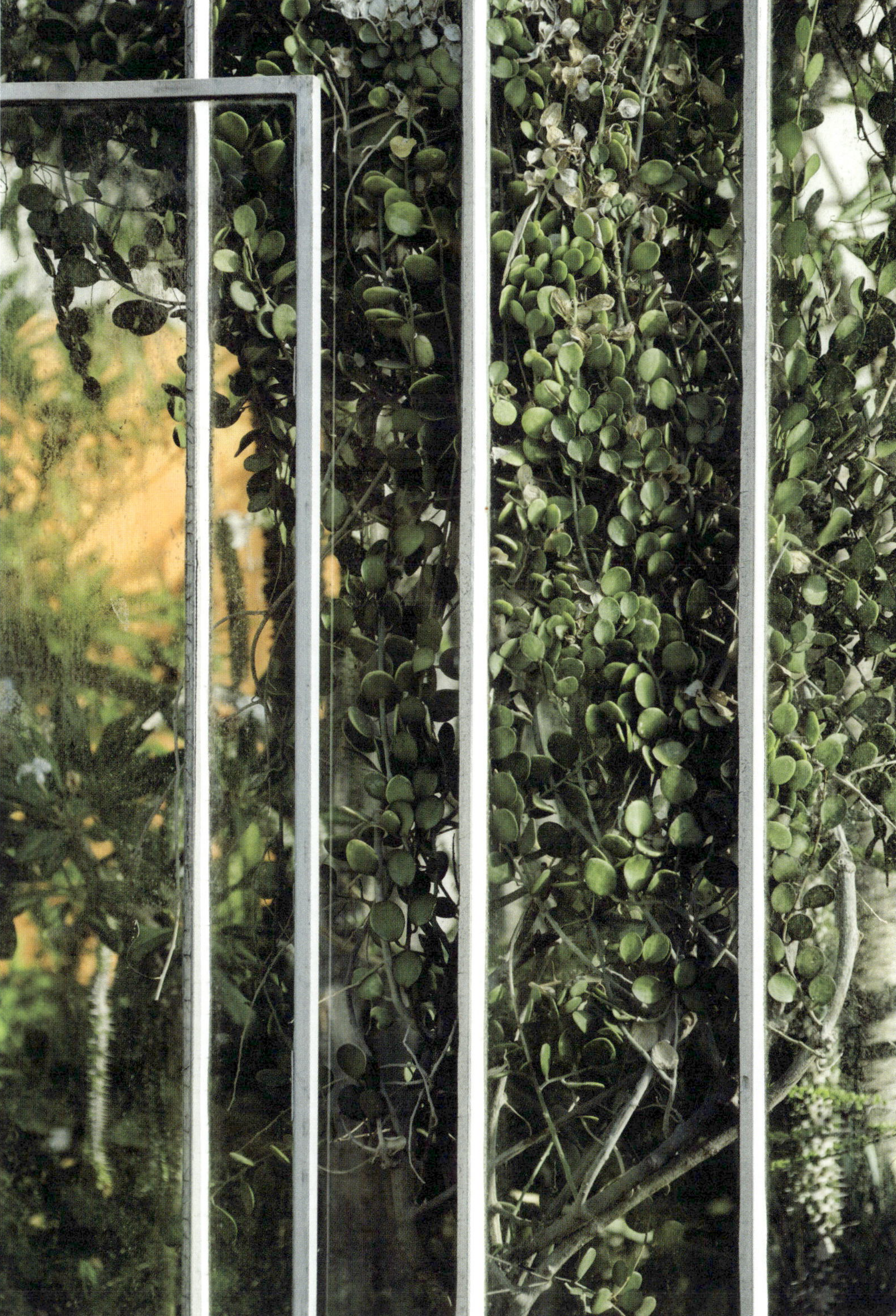

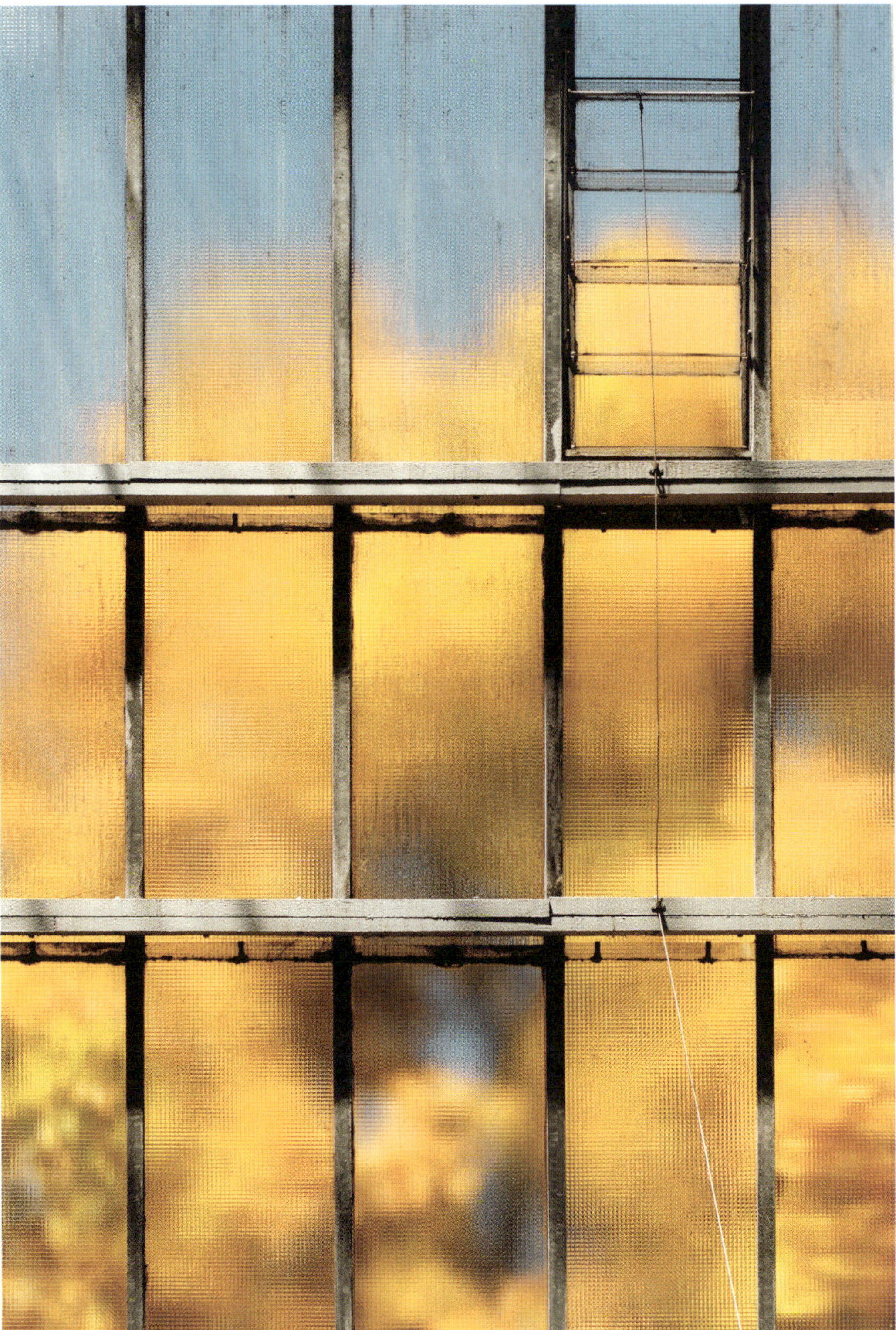

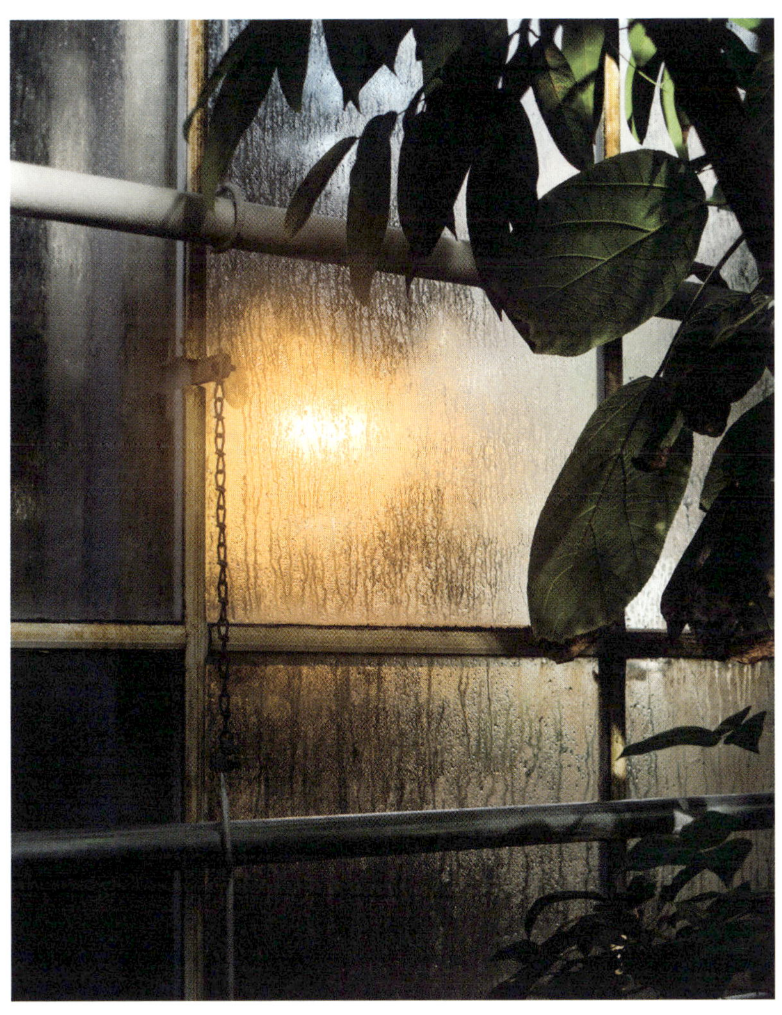

89   Amsterdam, Netherlands

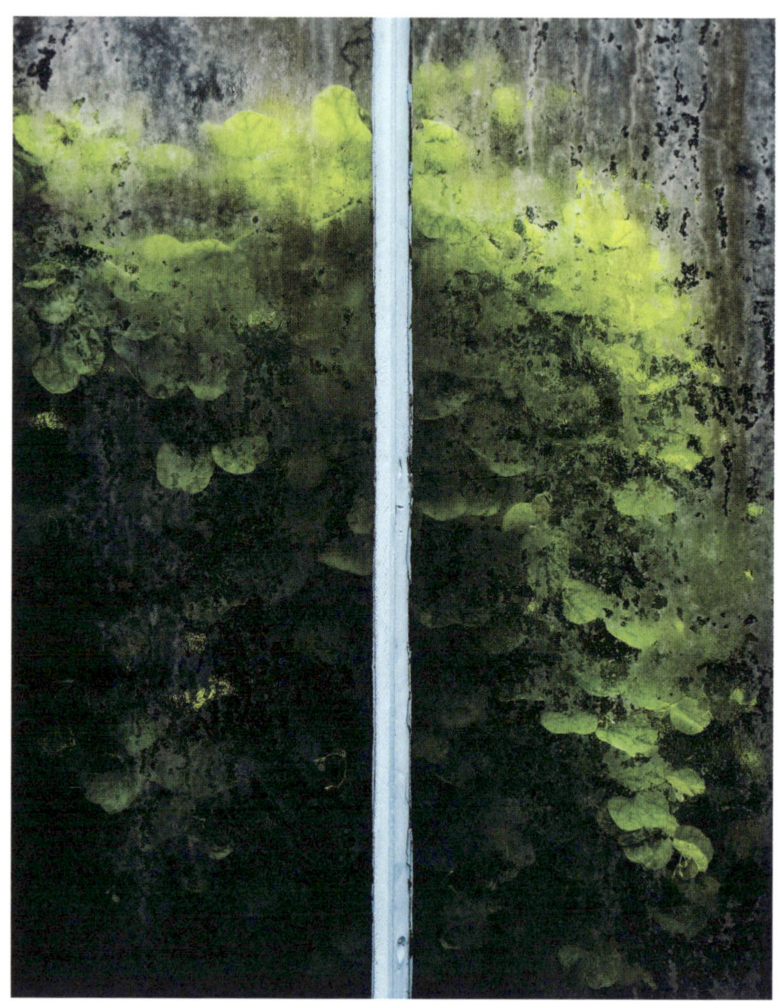

90   Paris, France

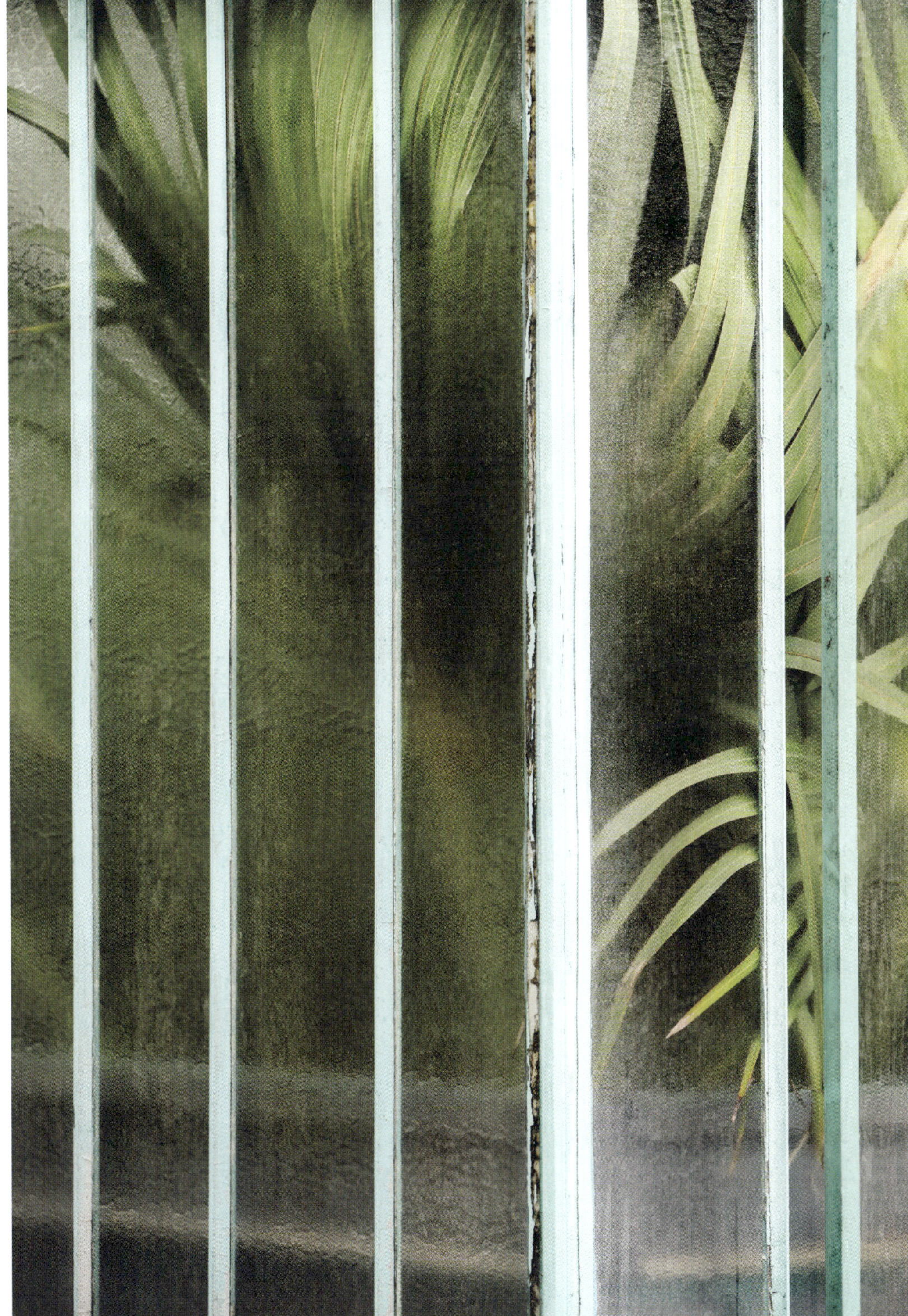

Geneva, Switzerland

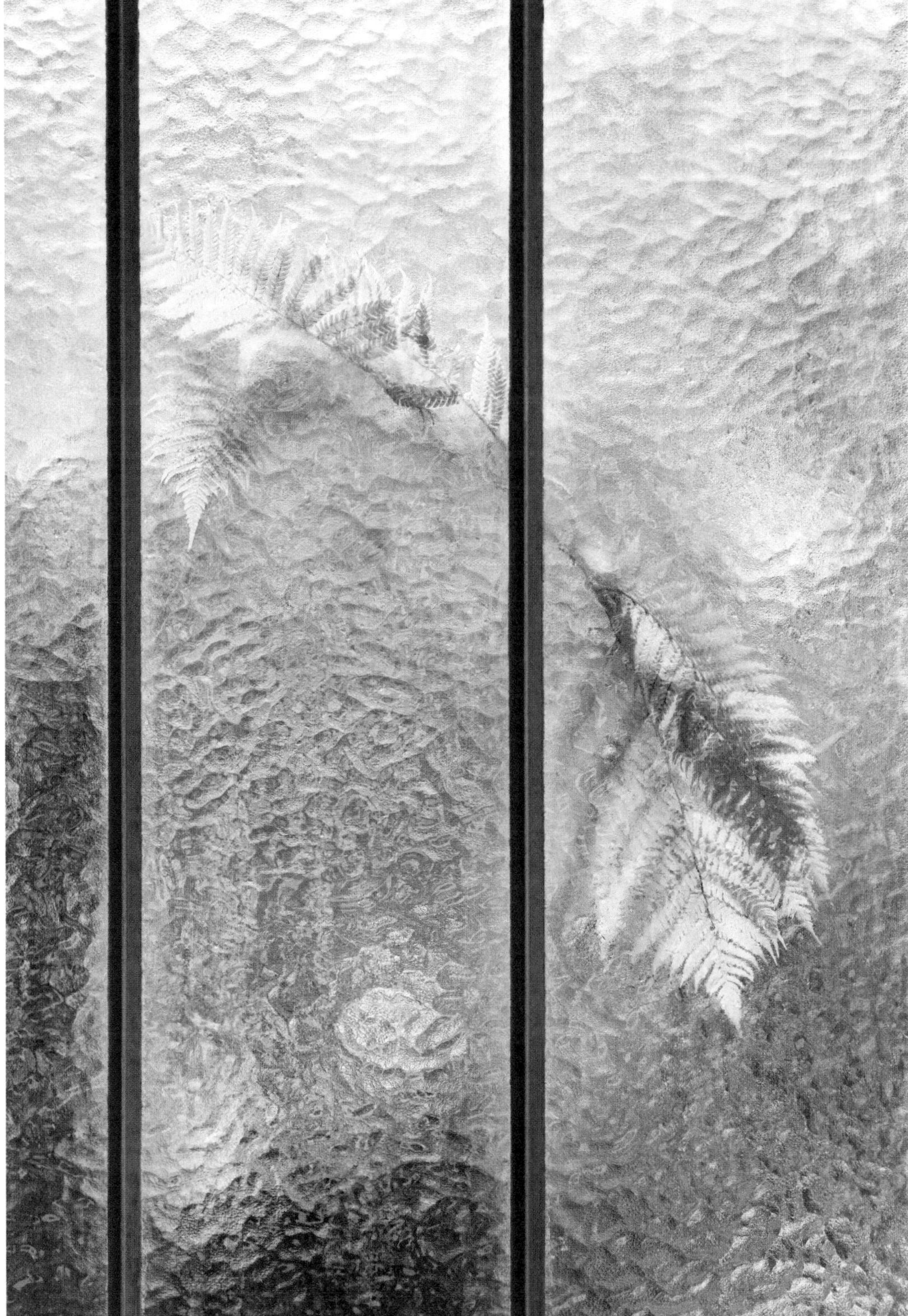

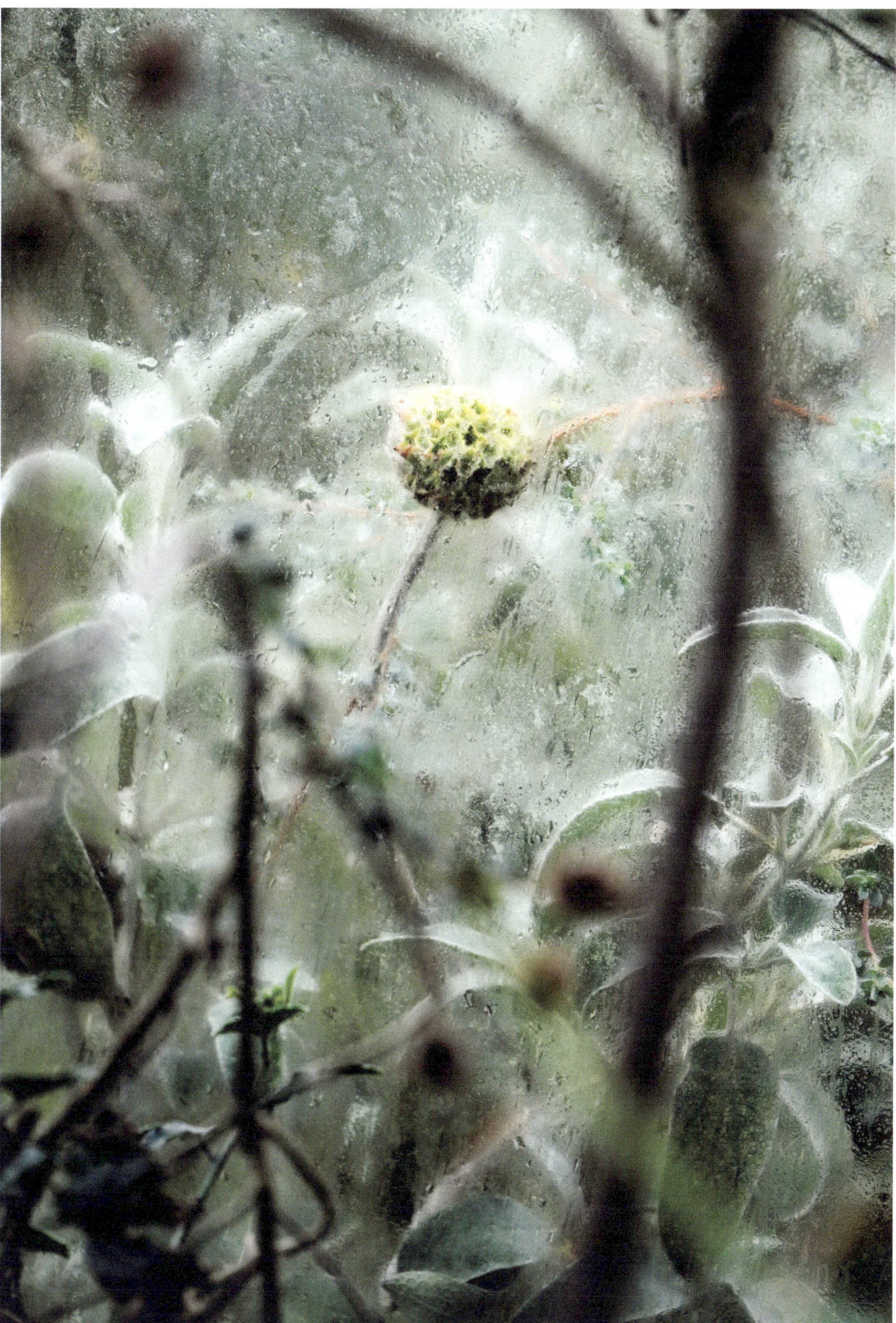

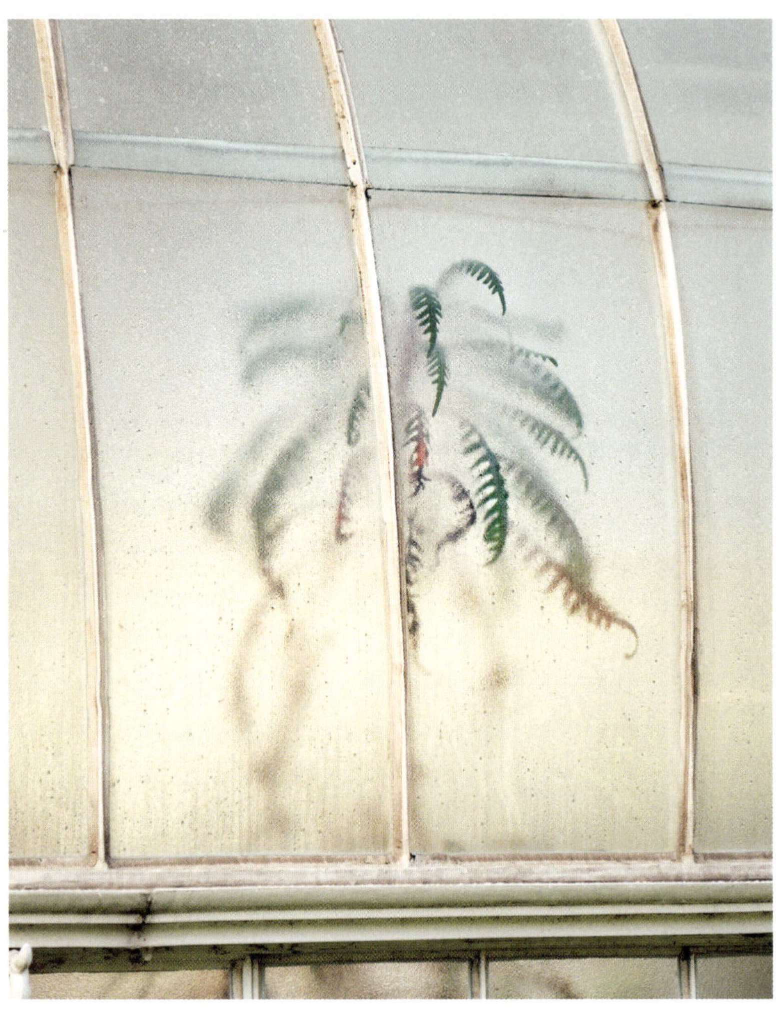

  Glasgow, Scotland *(above)* Lyon, France *(opposite)*

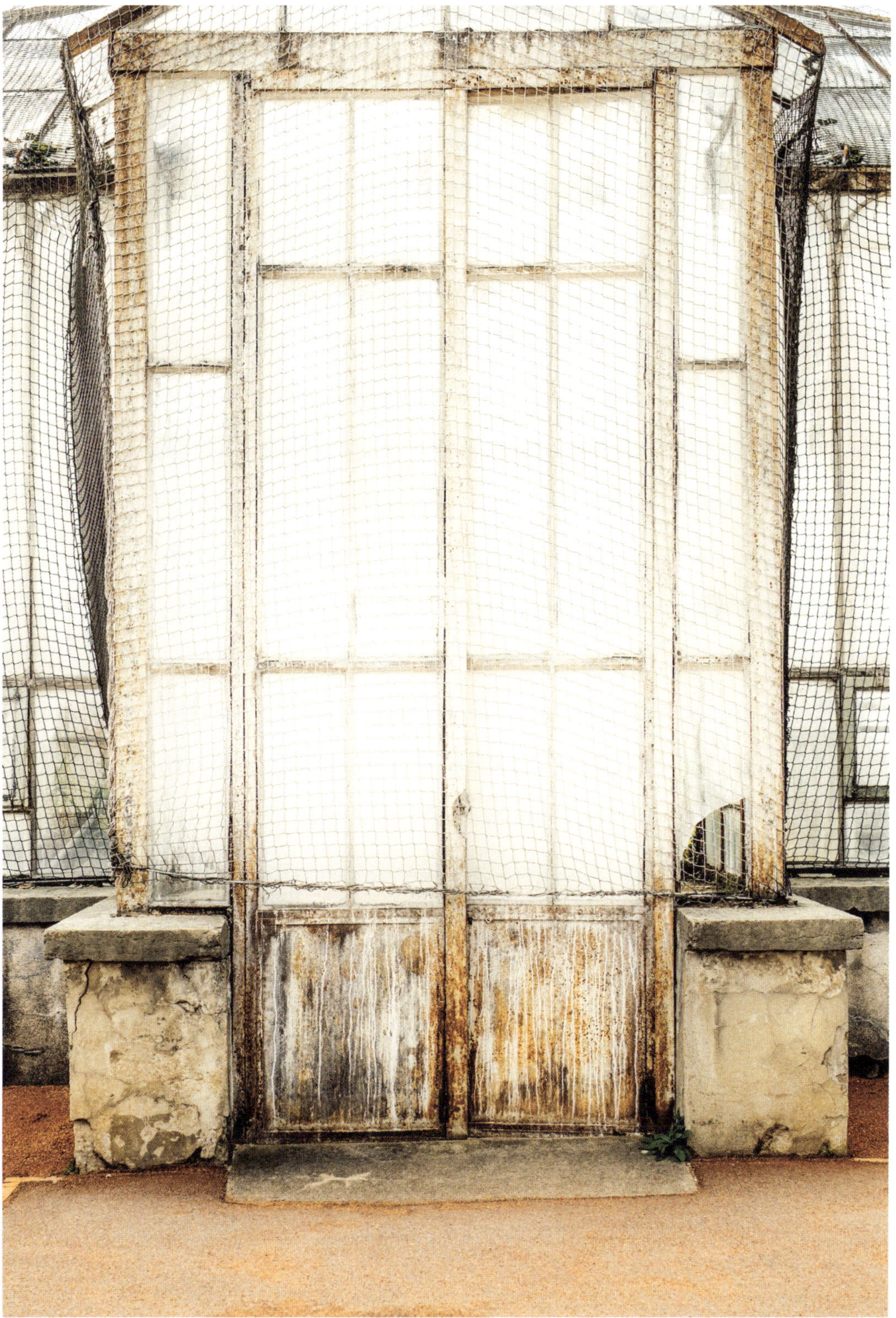

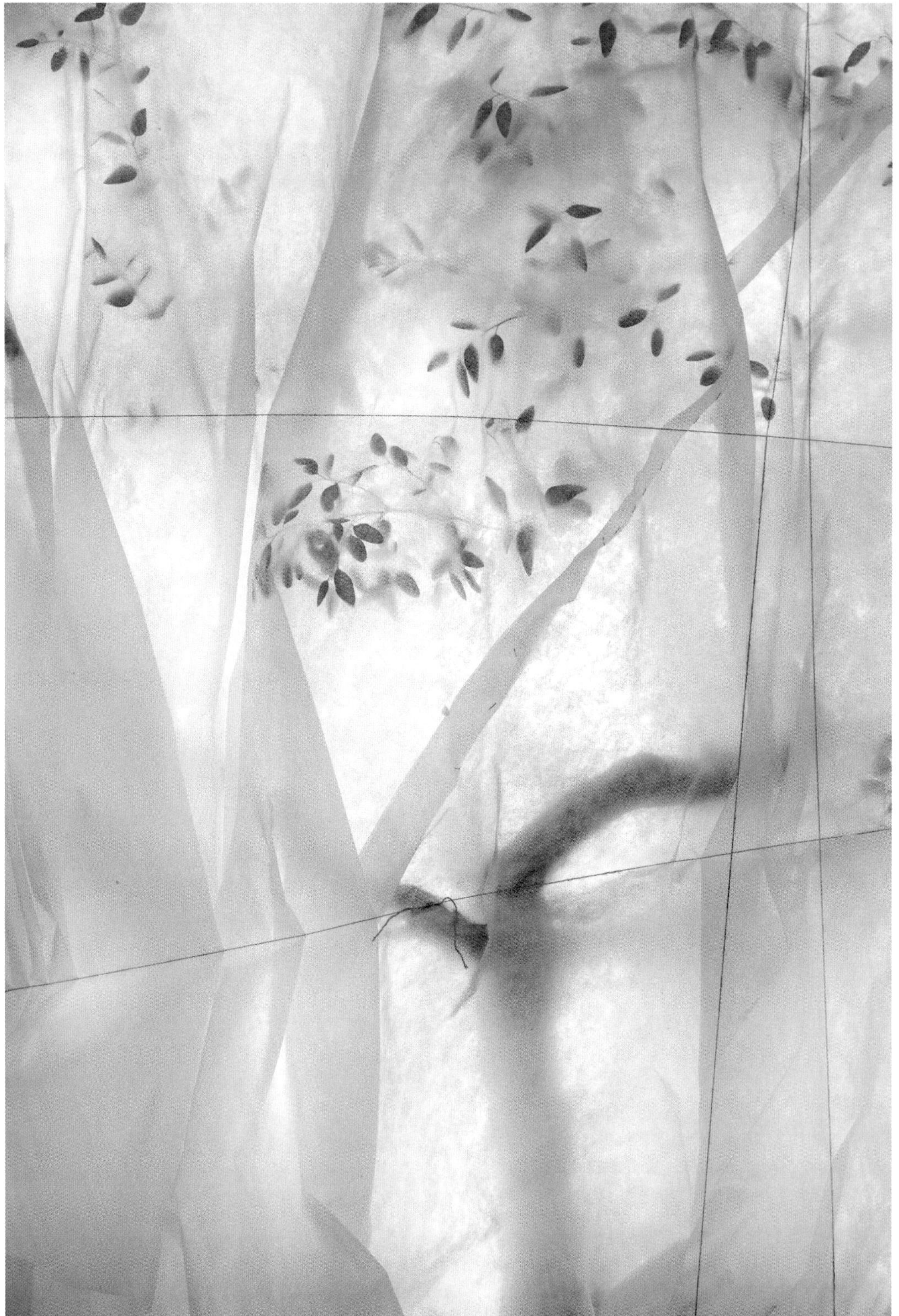

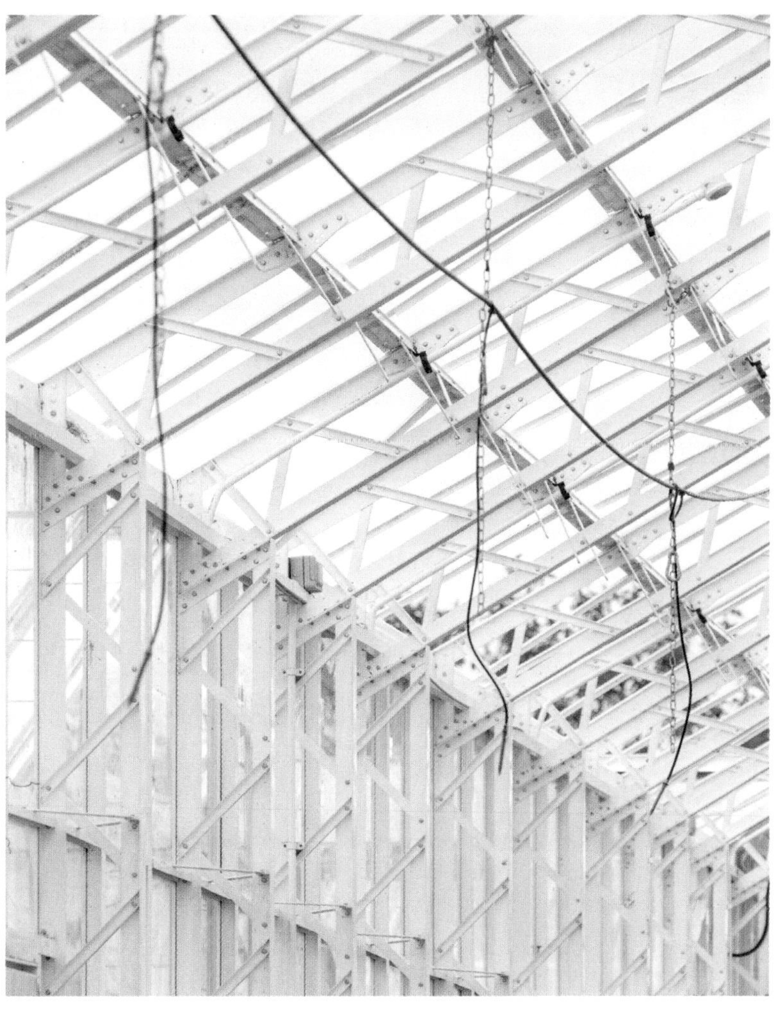

    Prague, Czech Republic *(opposite)* Aberdeen, Scotland *(above)*

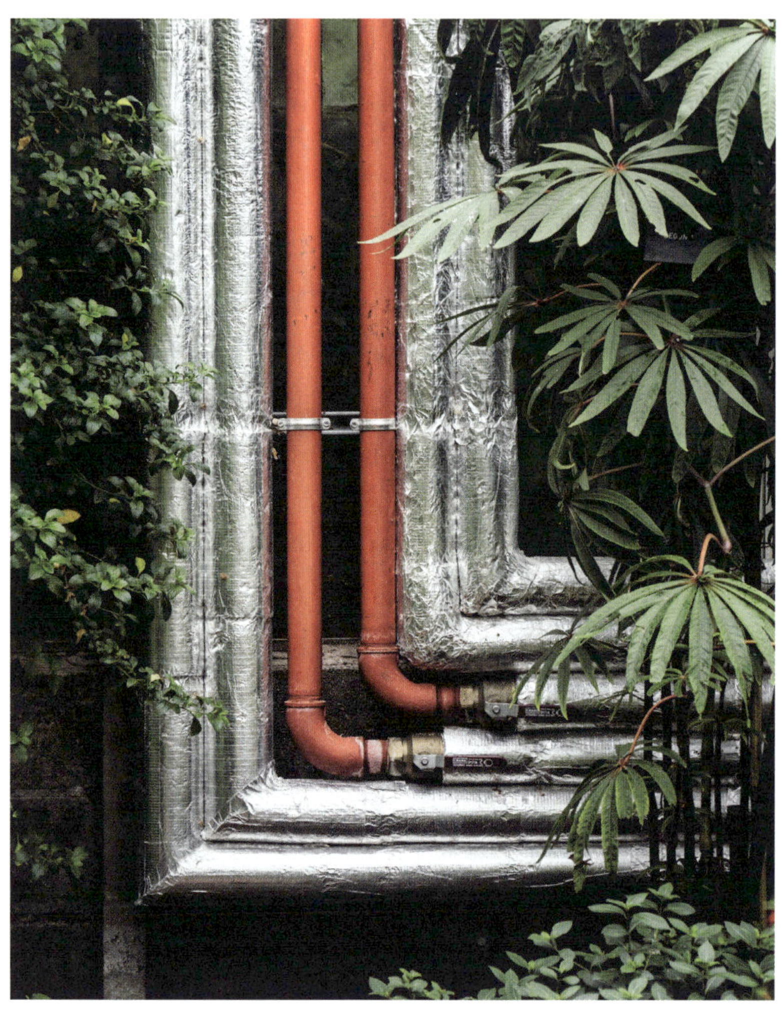

 Dundee, Scotland *(above)* Geneva, Switzerland *(opposite)*

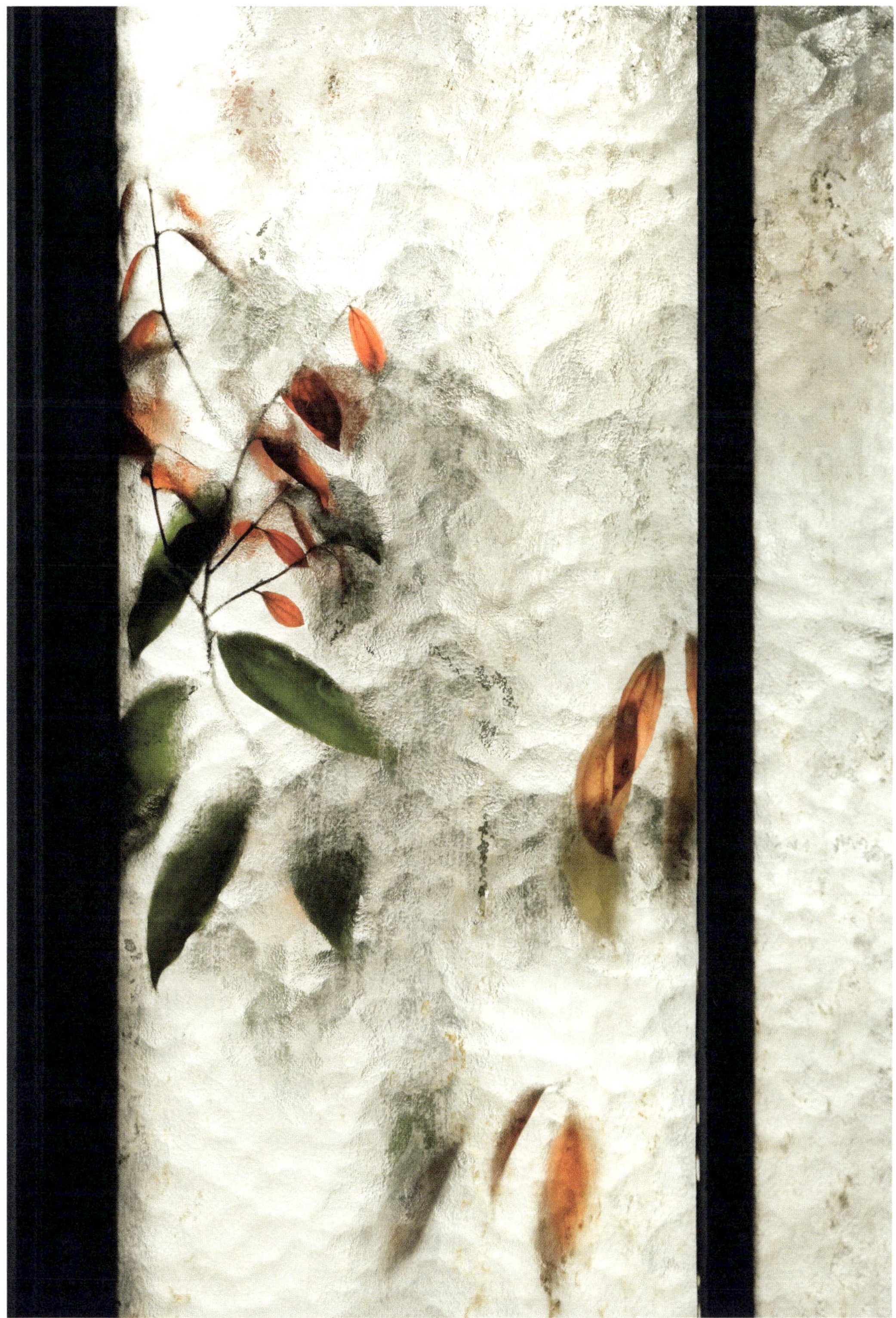

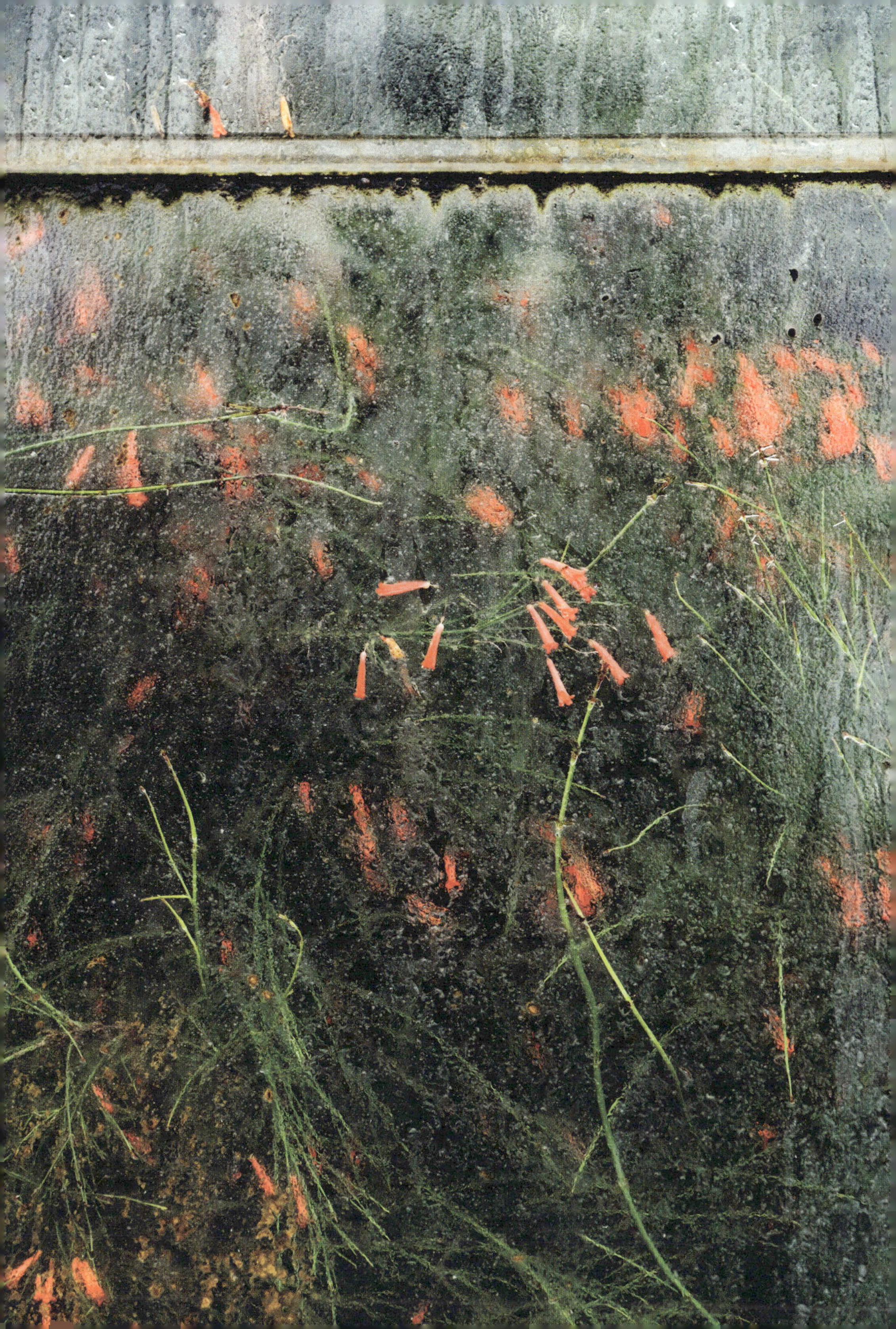

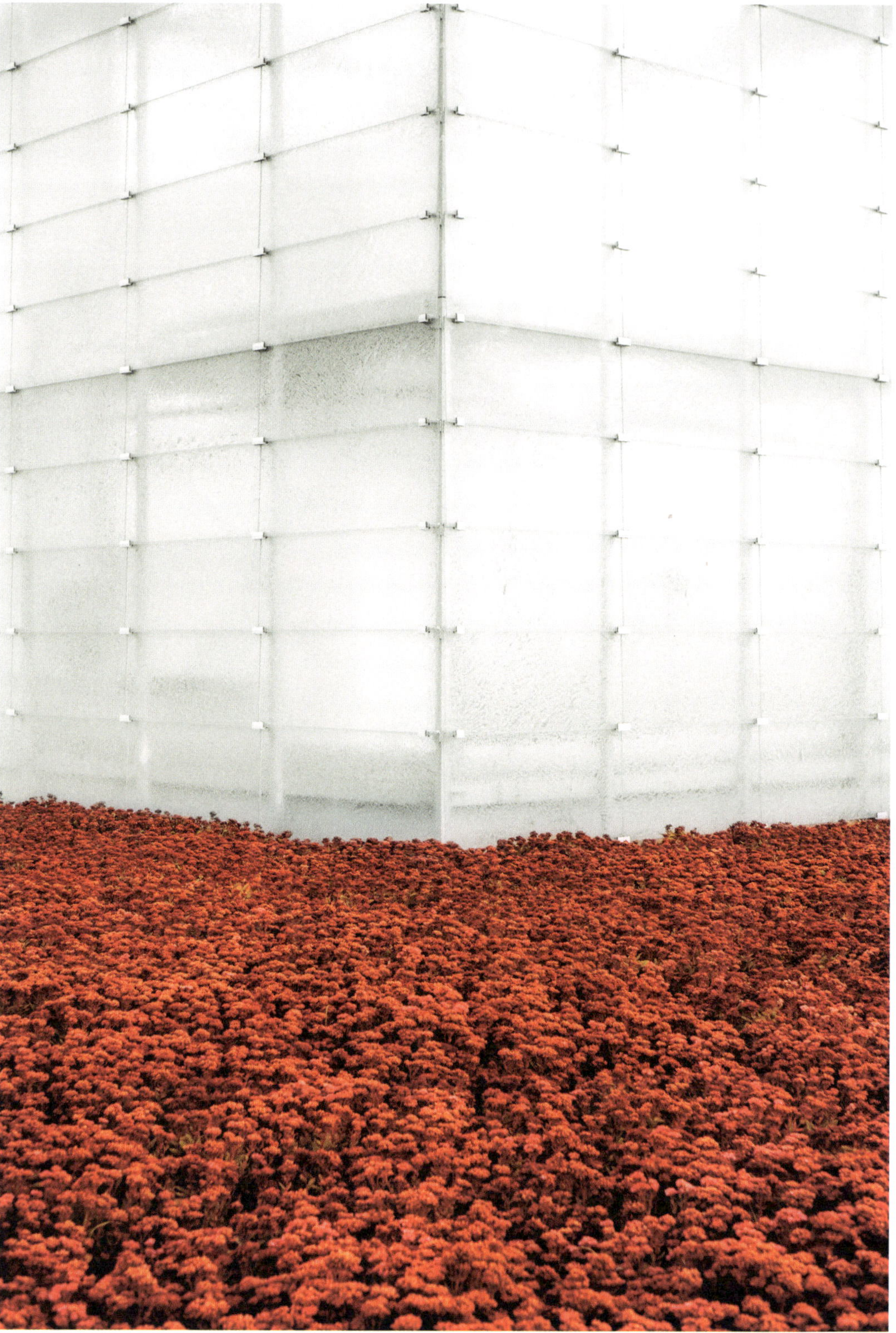

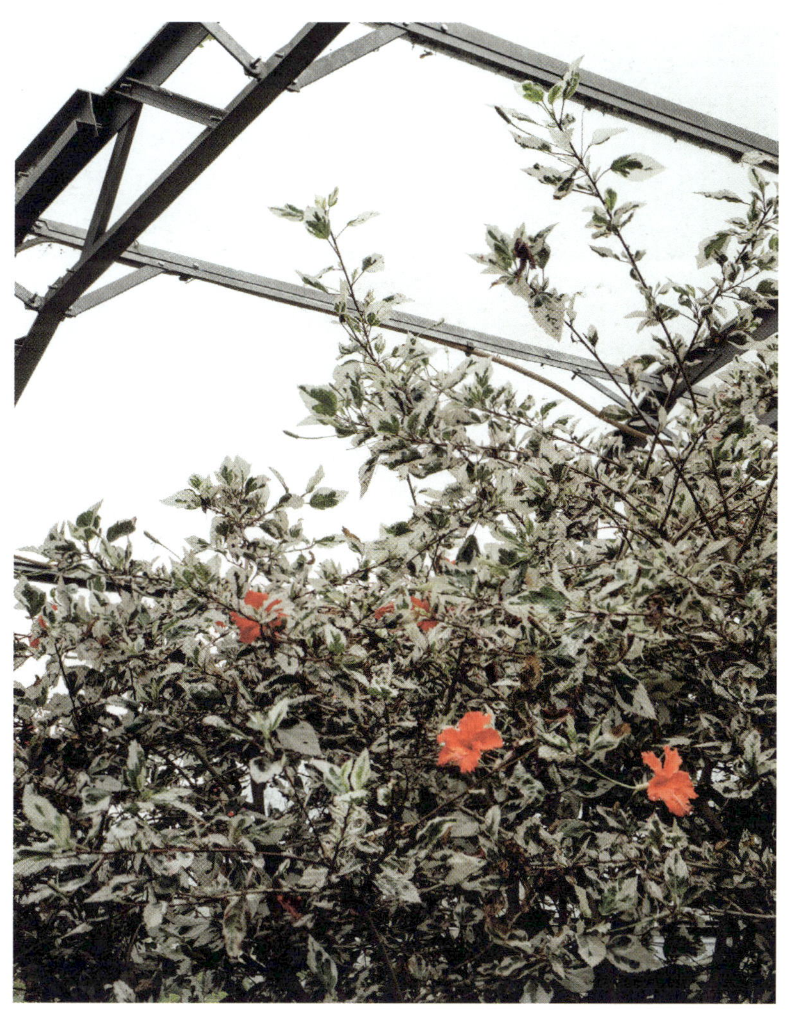

 Katowice, Poland *(opposite)* Aberdeen, Scotland *(above)*

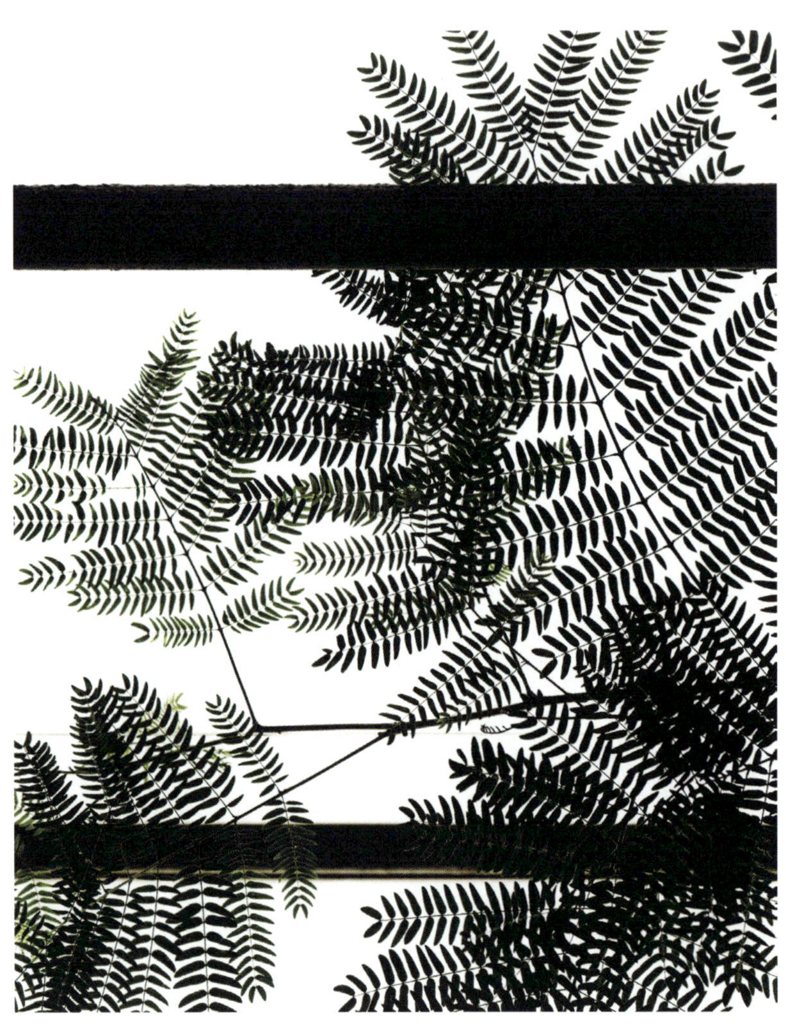

    Warsaw, Poland *(above & opposite)* Glasgow, Scotland *(overleaf)*

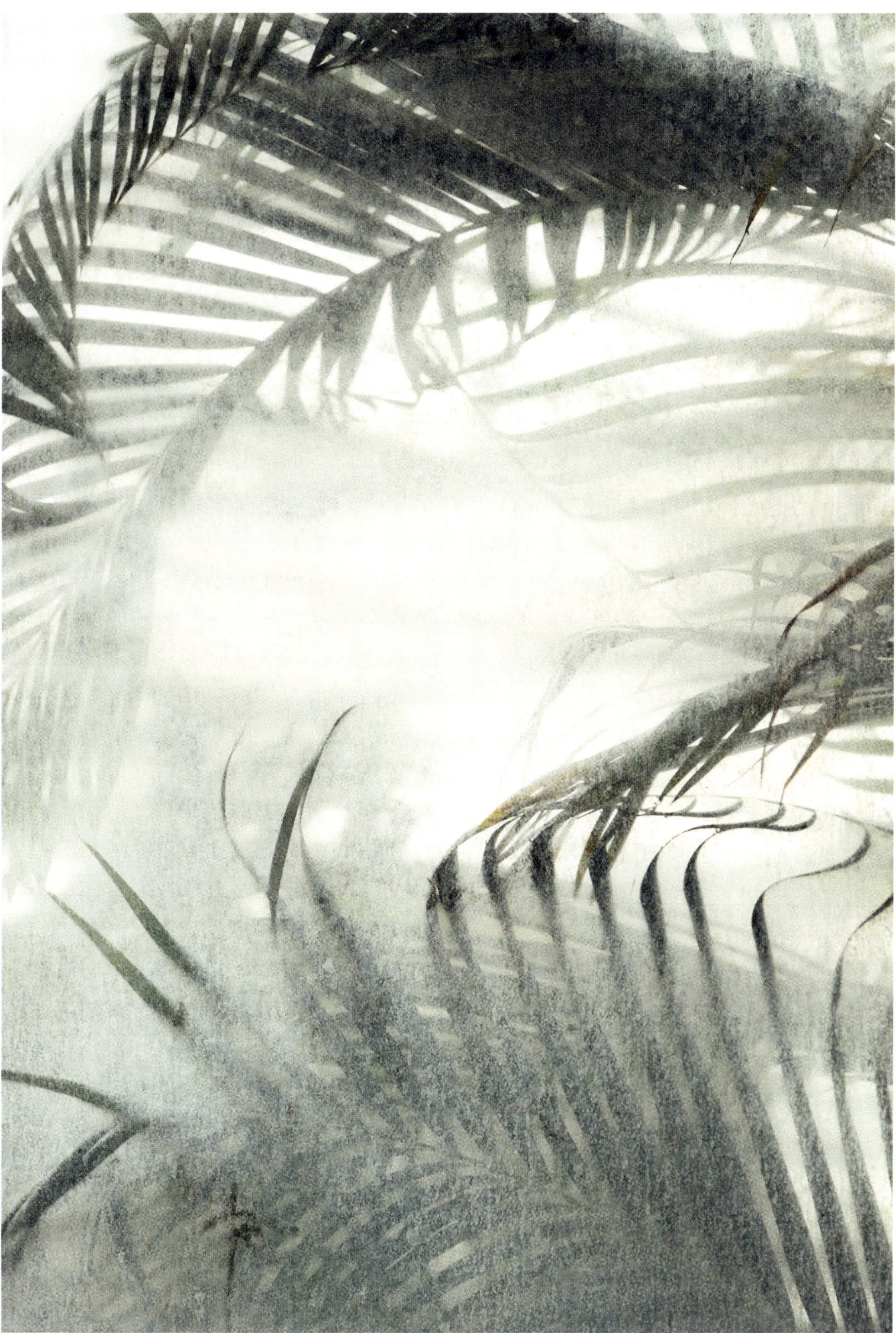

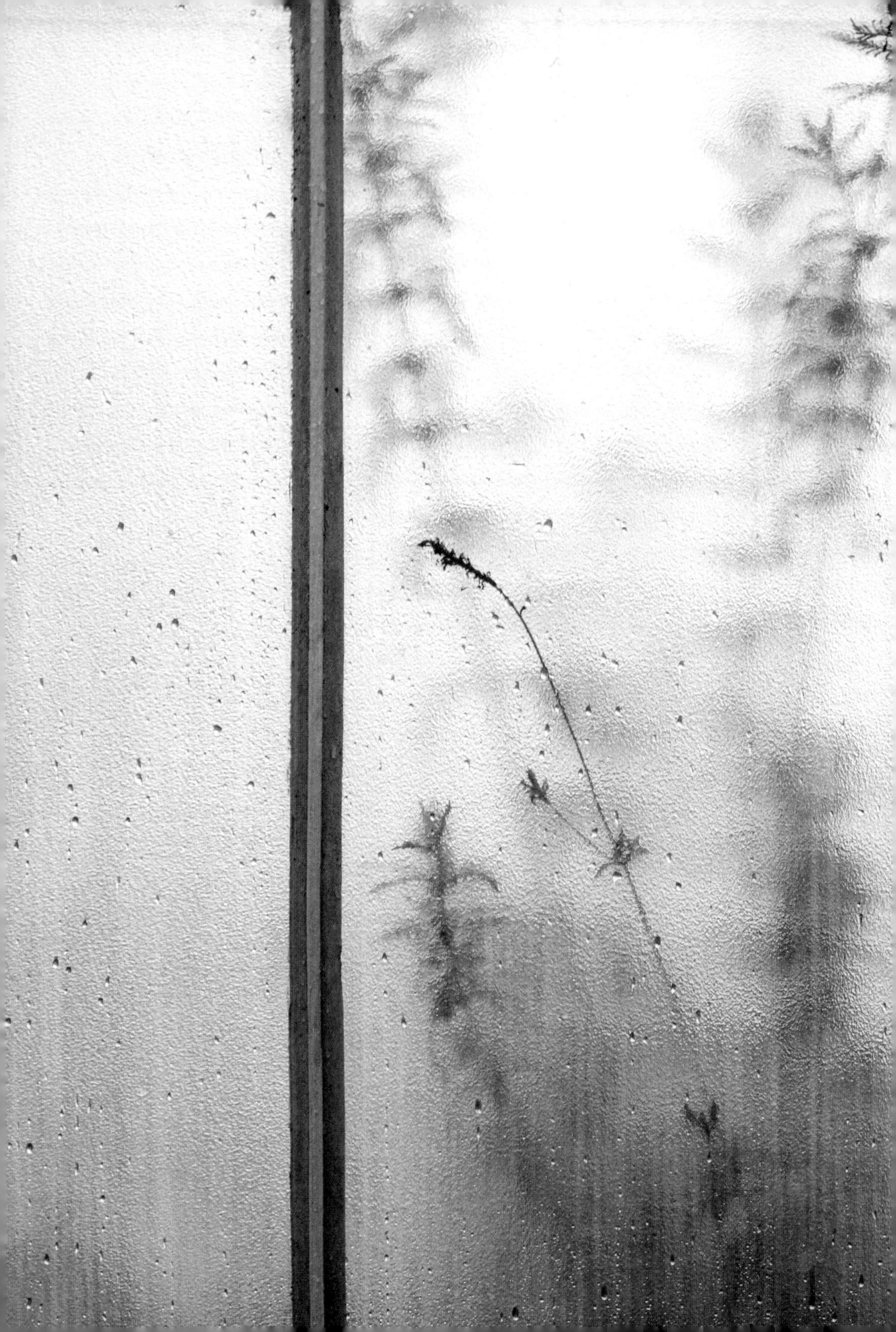

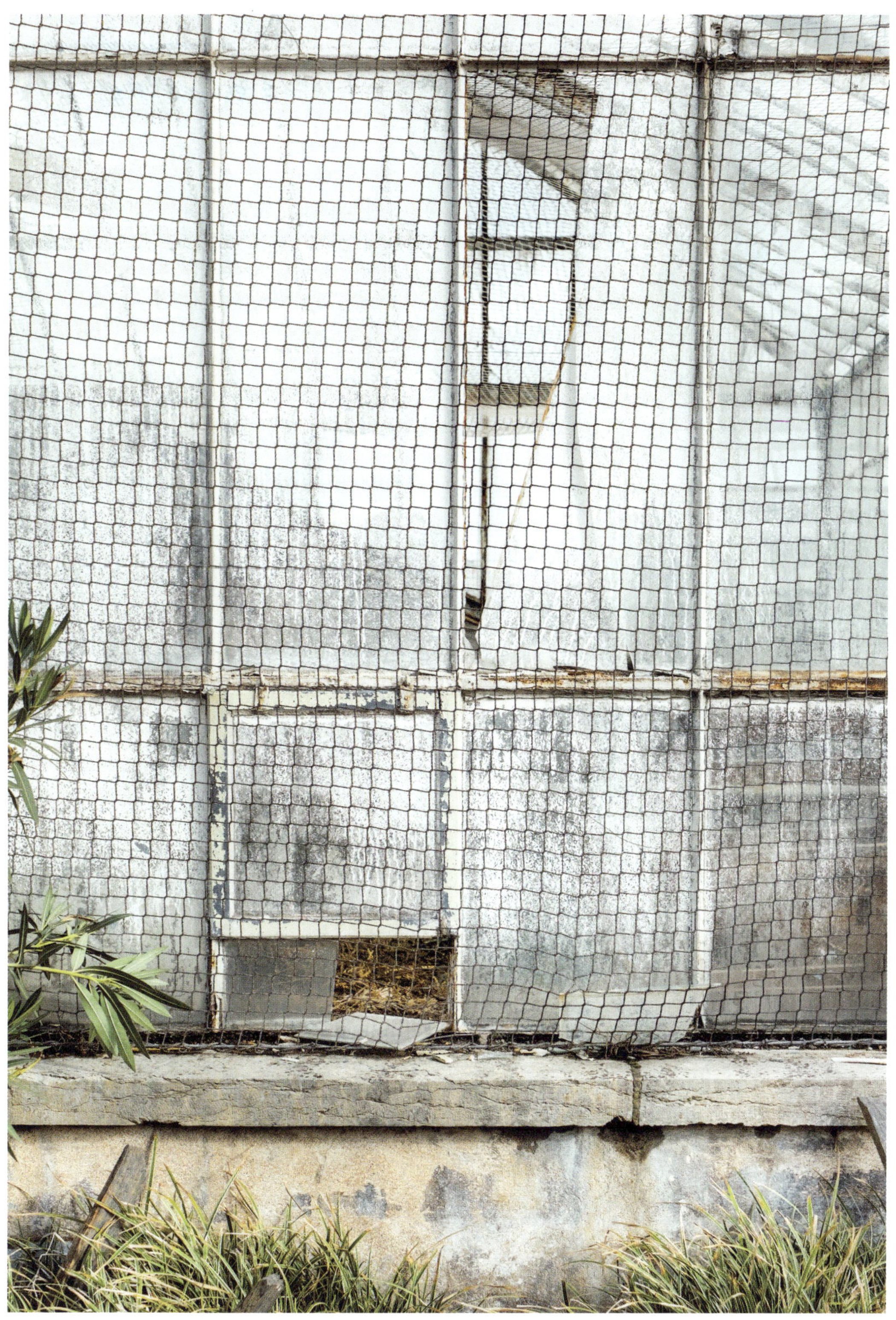

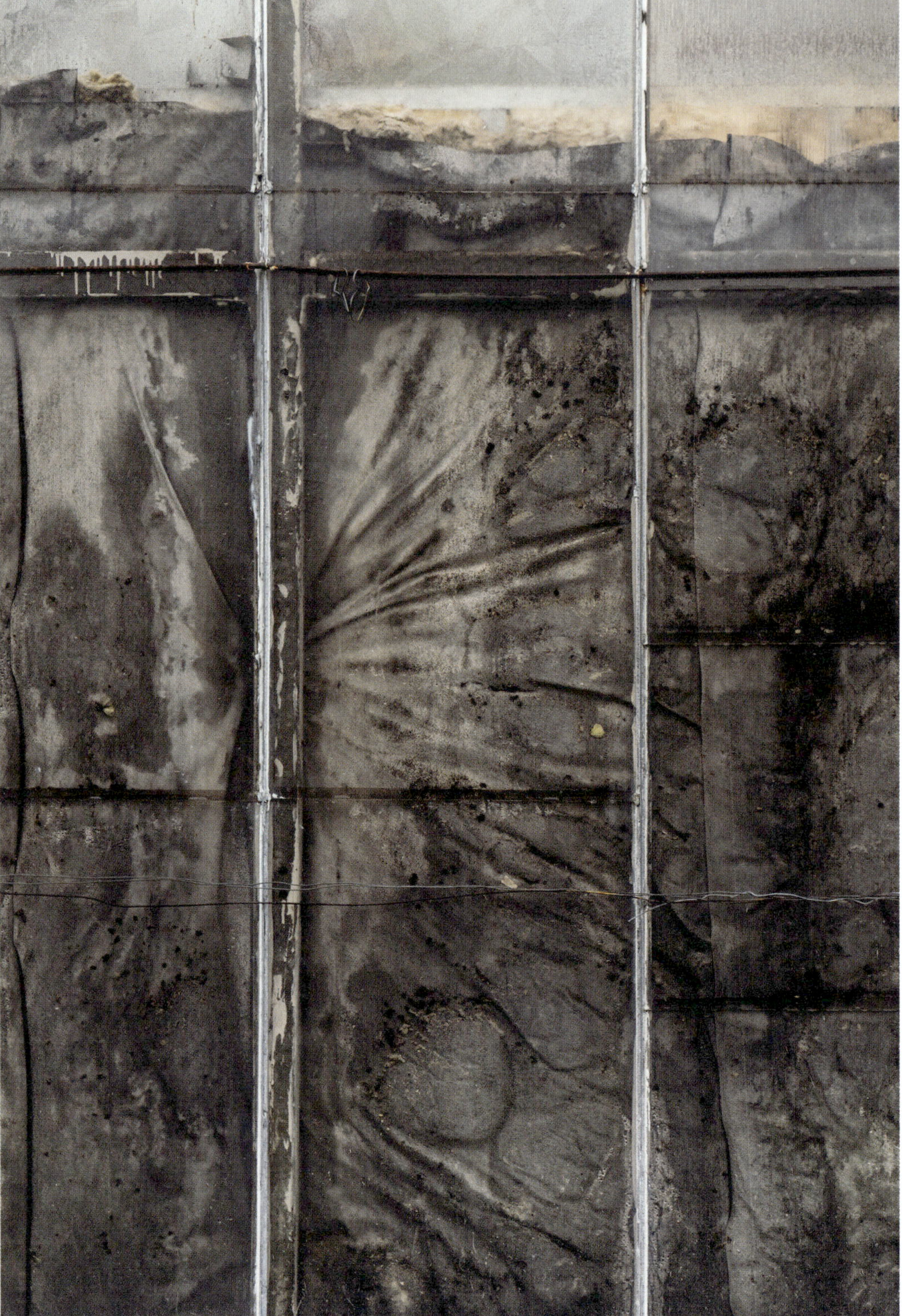

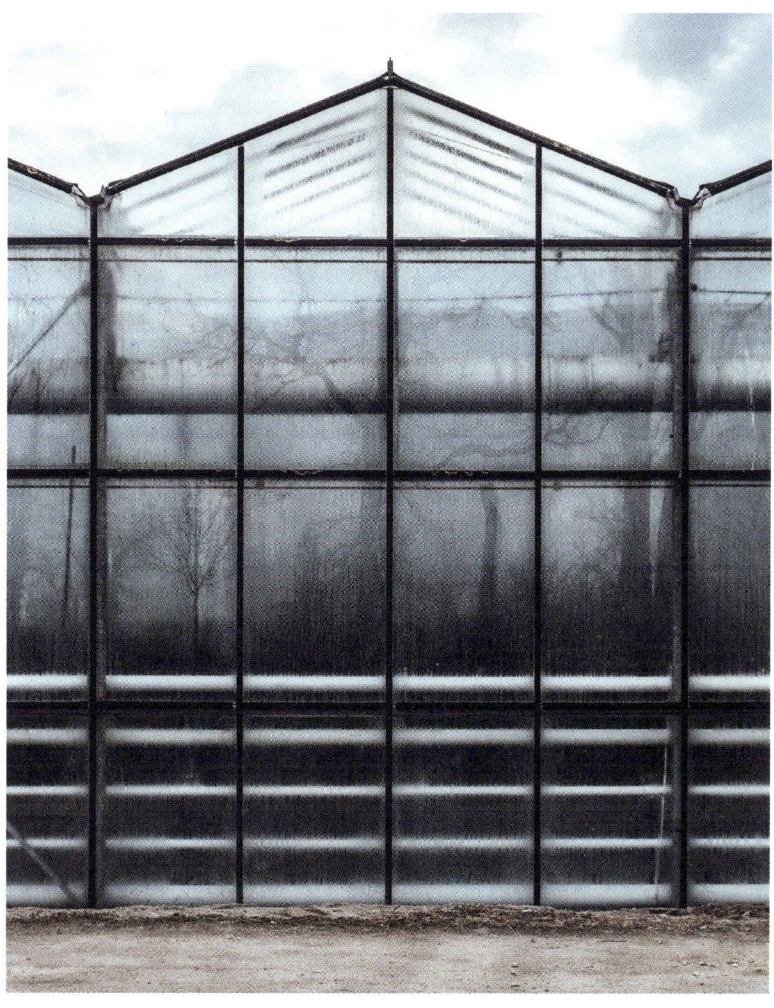

  Warsaw, Poland *(opposite)* Near Geneva, Switzerland *(above)*

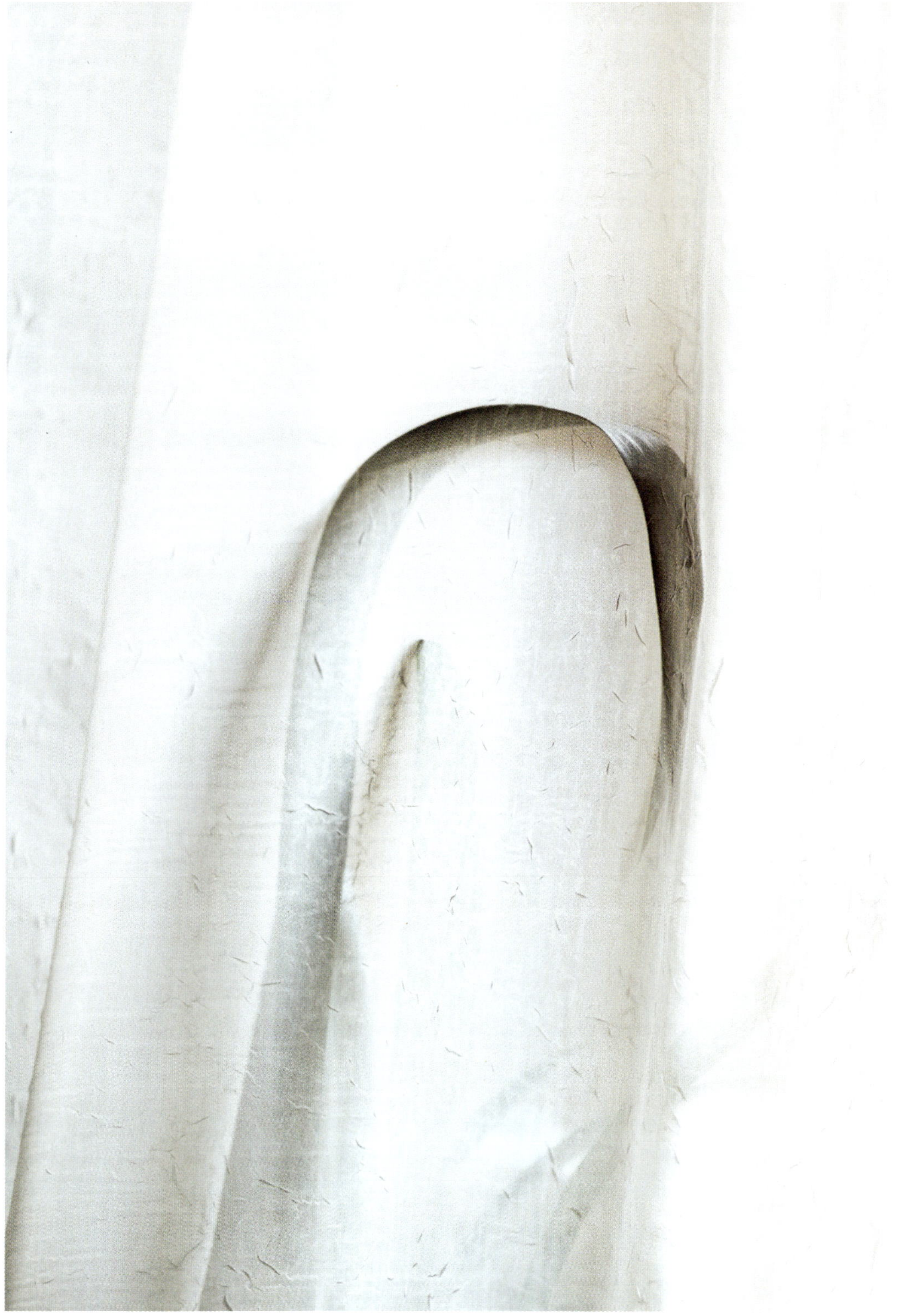

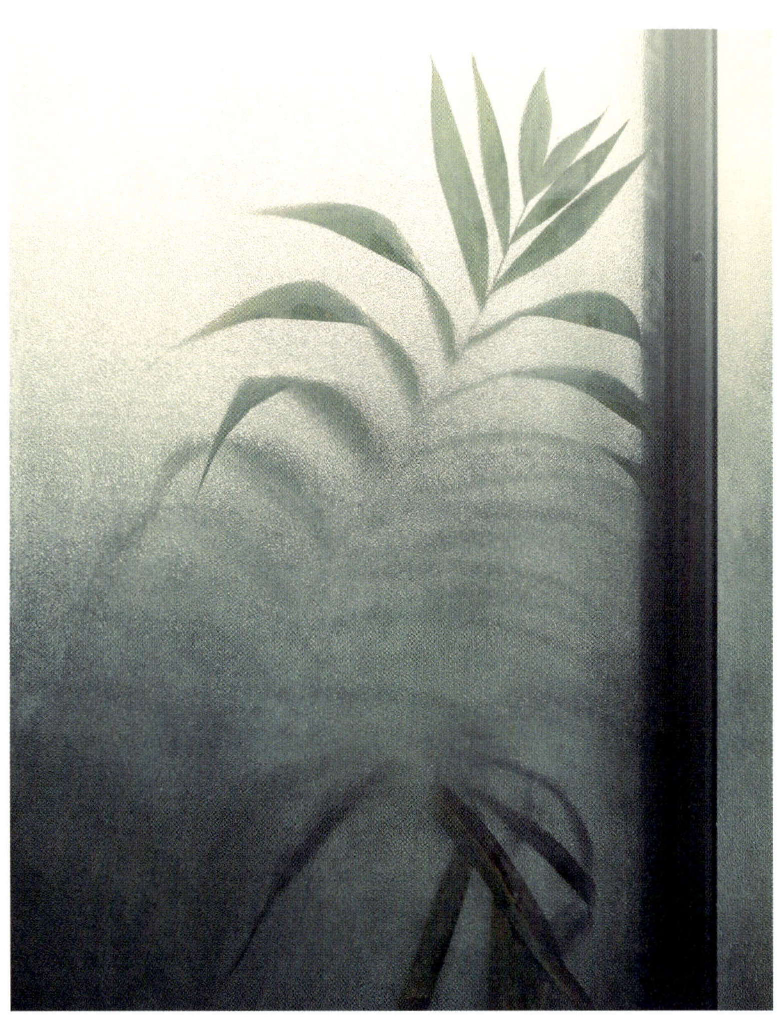

116   Glasgow, Scotland *(above)* Lyon, France *(opposite)*

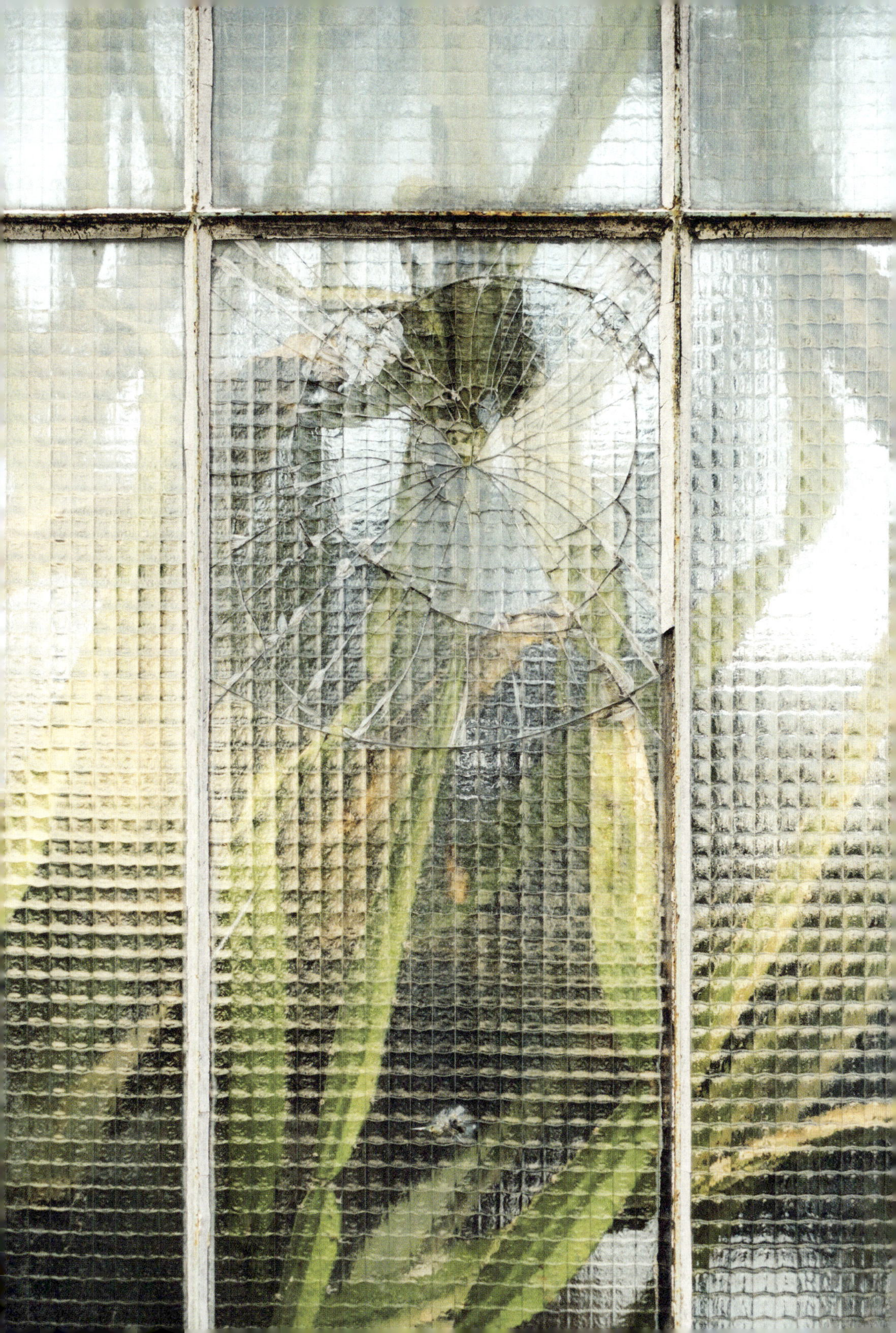

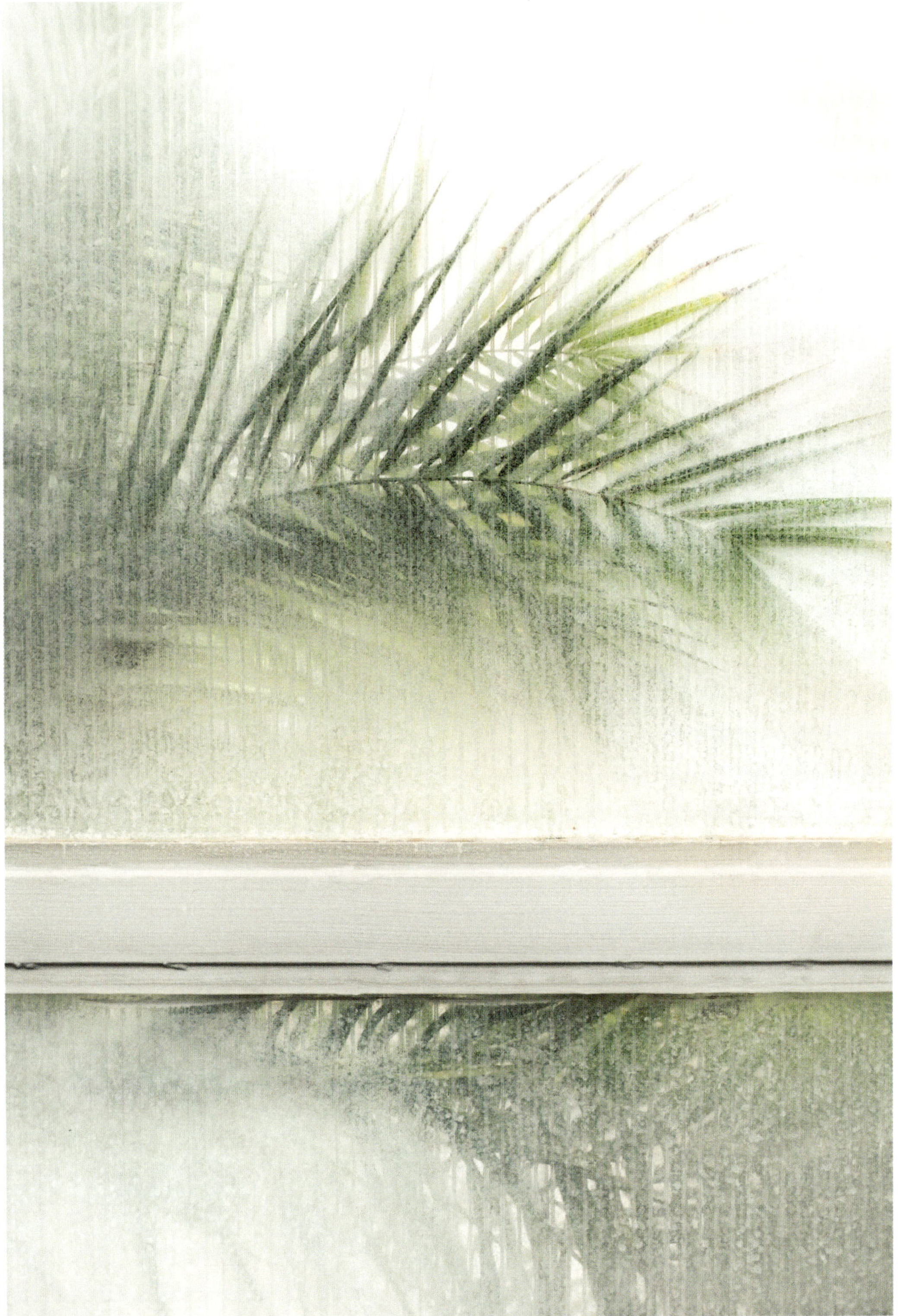

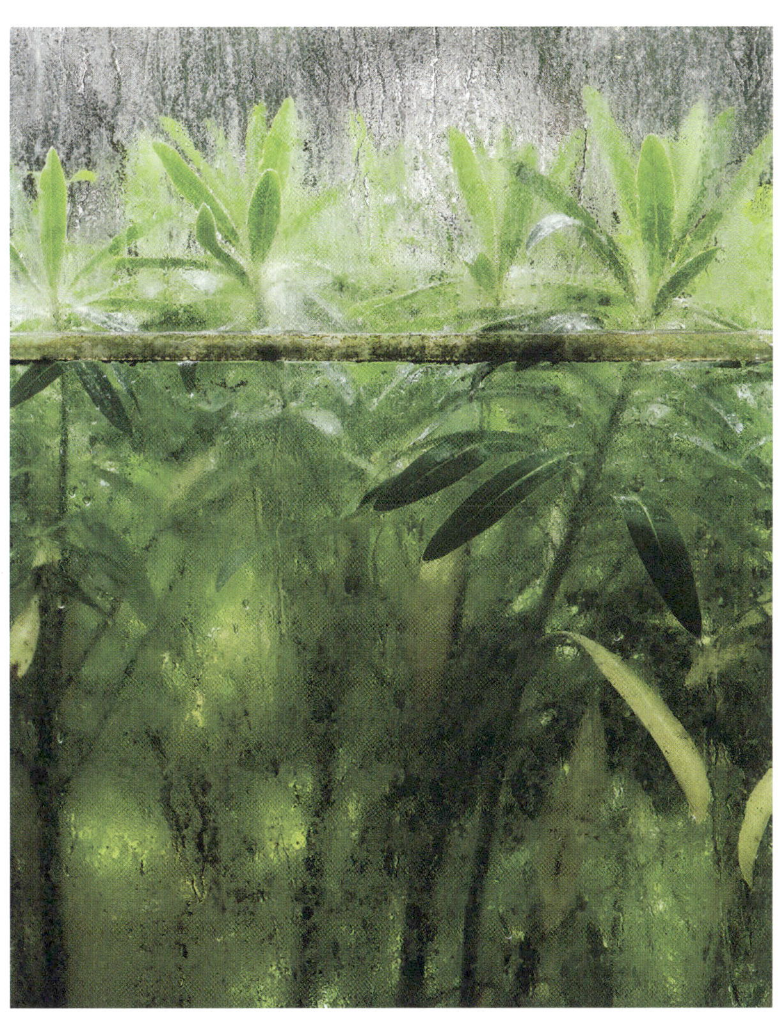

119   Brno, Czech Republic *(opposite)* Dundee, Scotland *(above)*

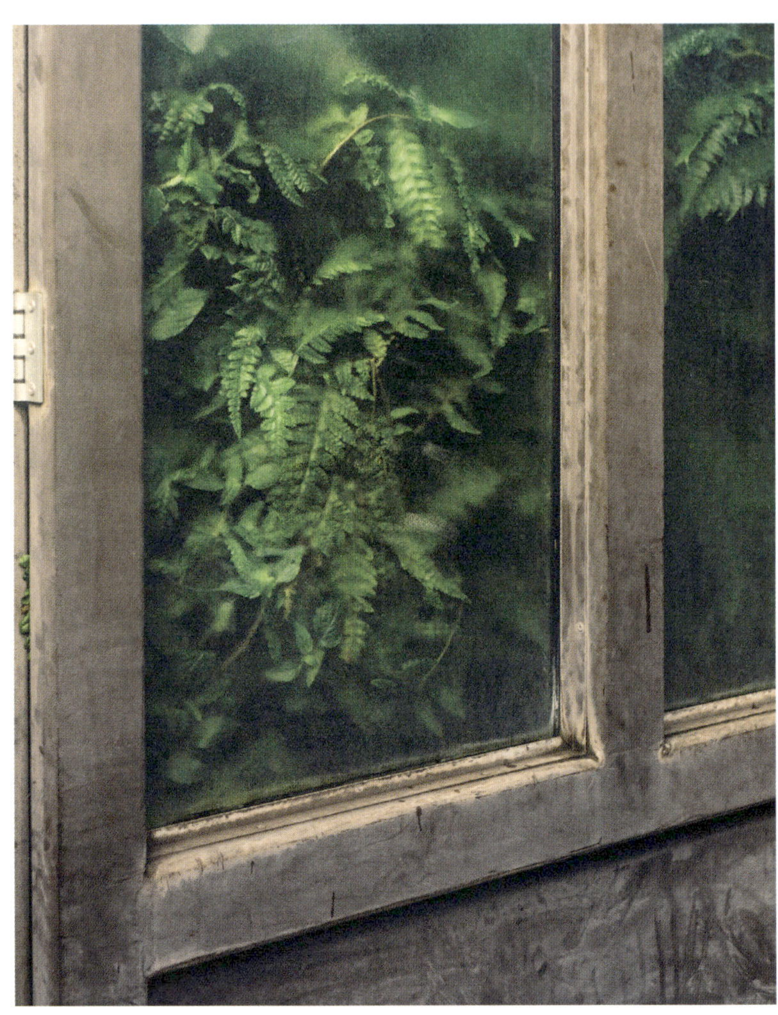

120   Glasgow, Scotland *(above)* Nantes, France *(opposite)*

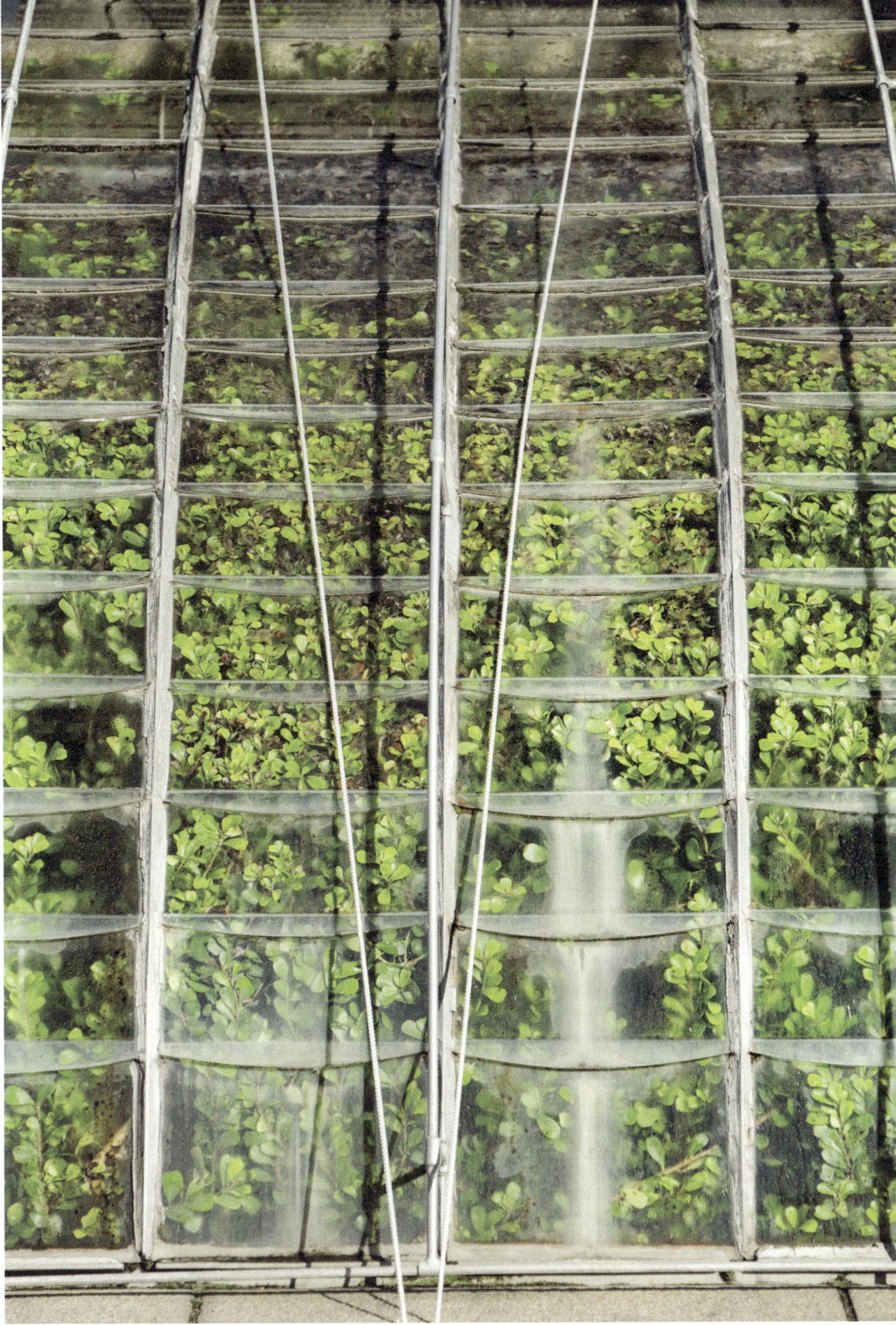

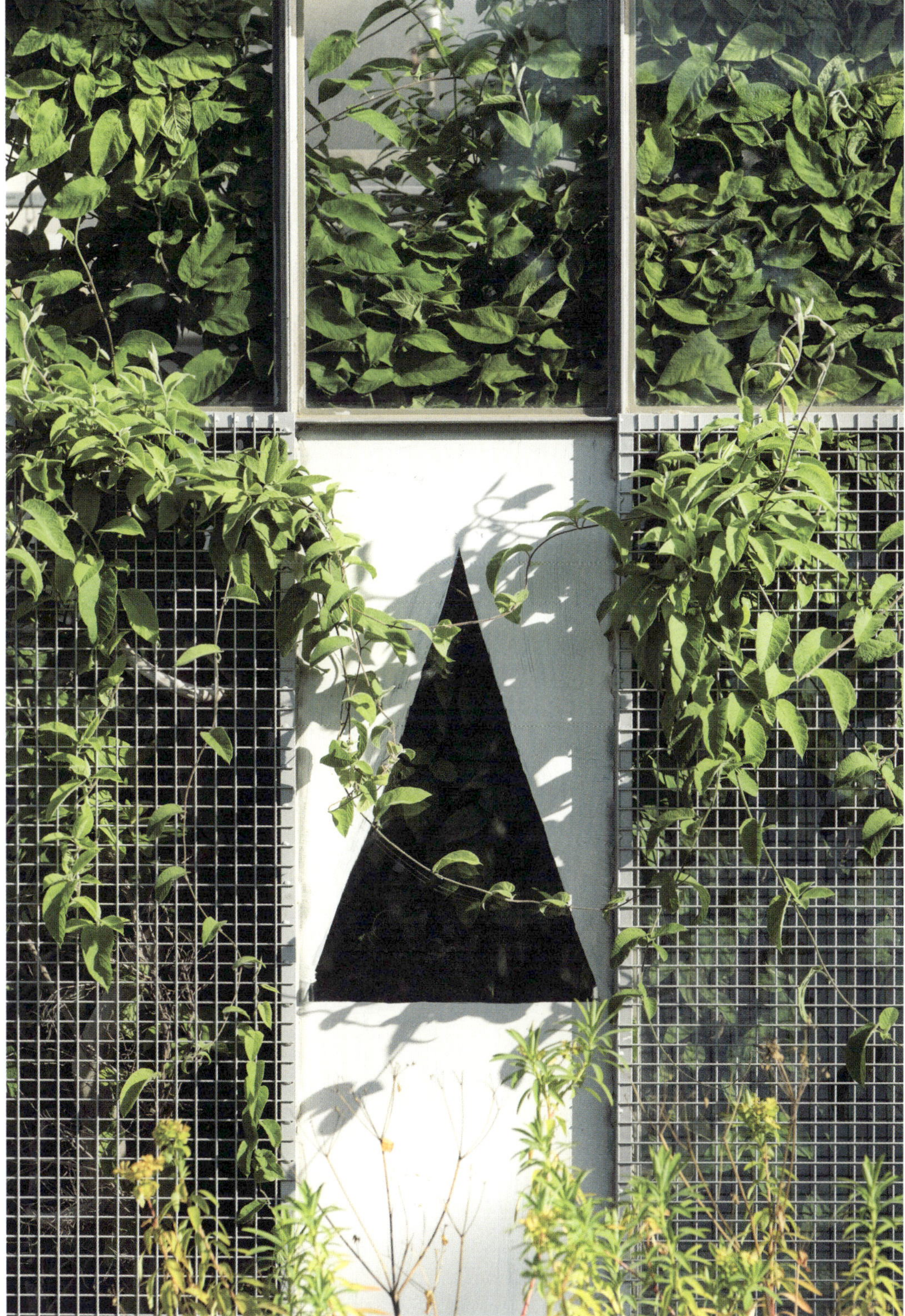

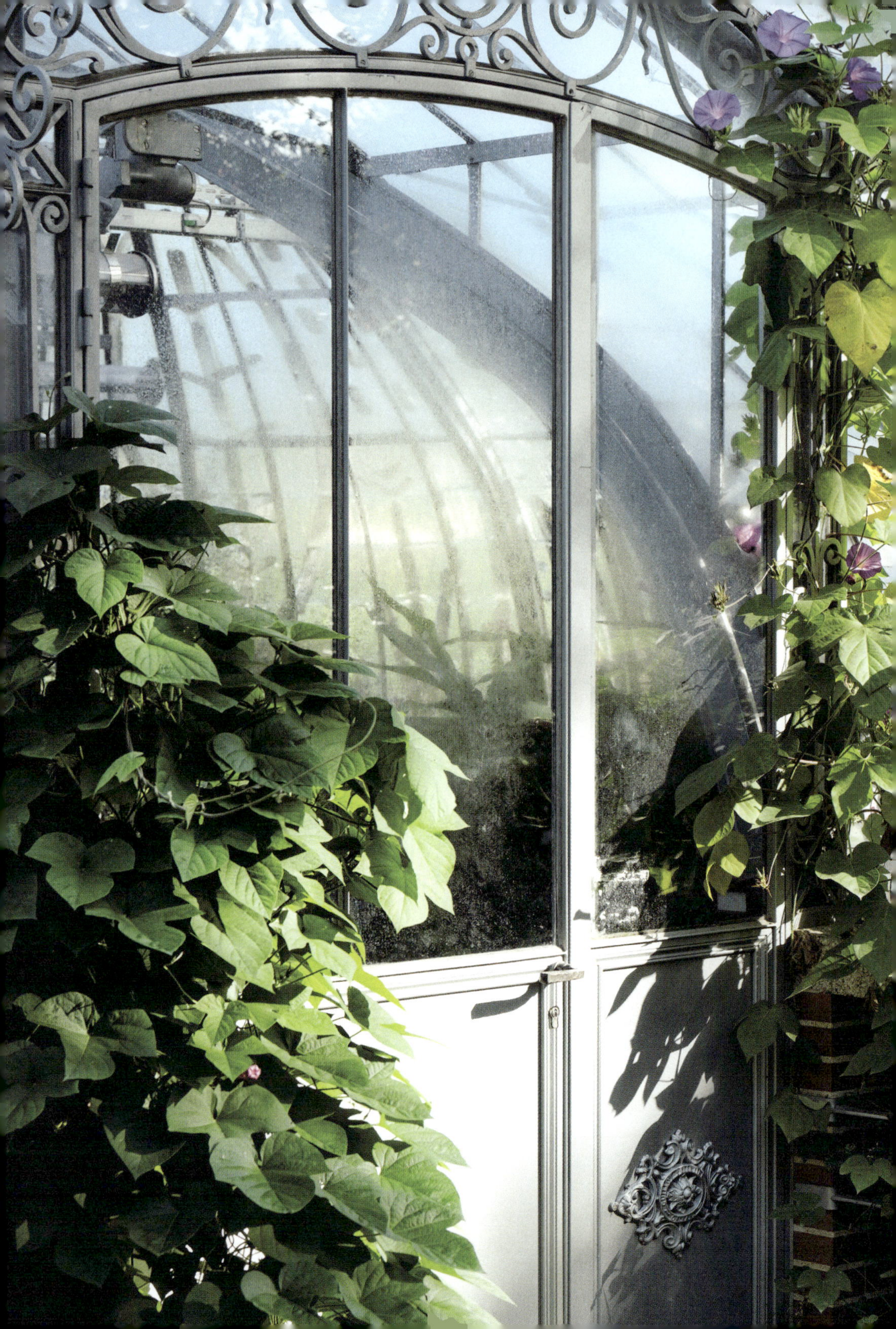

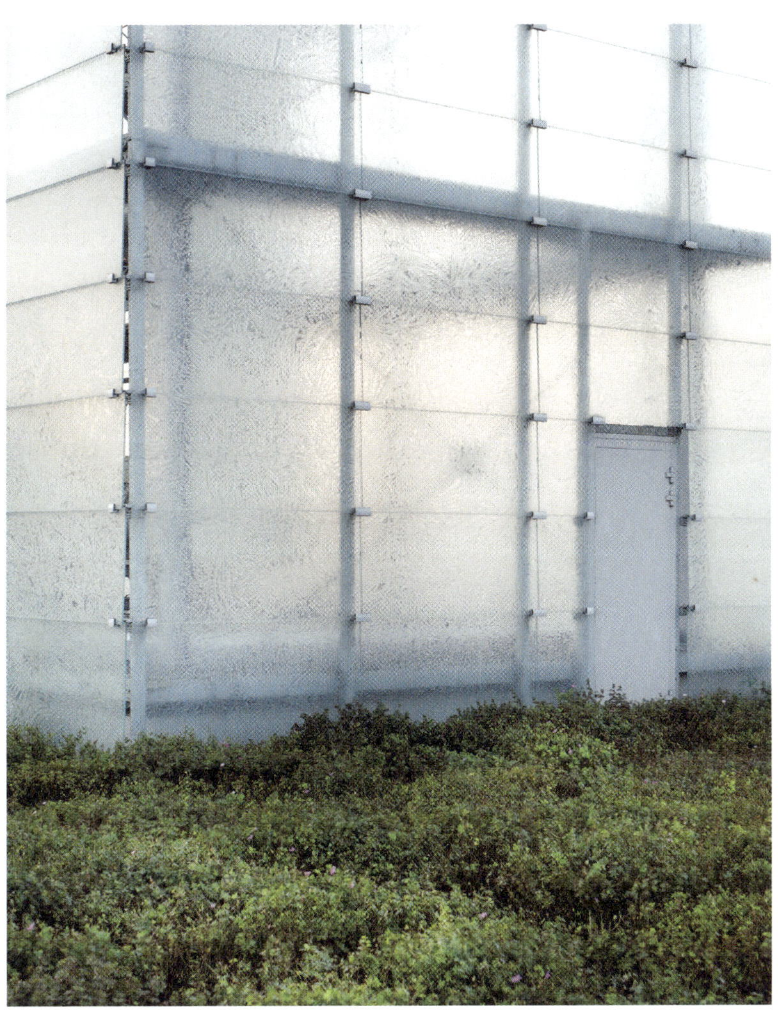

Nantes, France *(opposite)* Katowice, Poland *(above)*
Paris, France *(overleaf)*

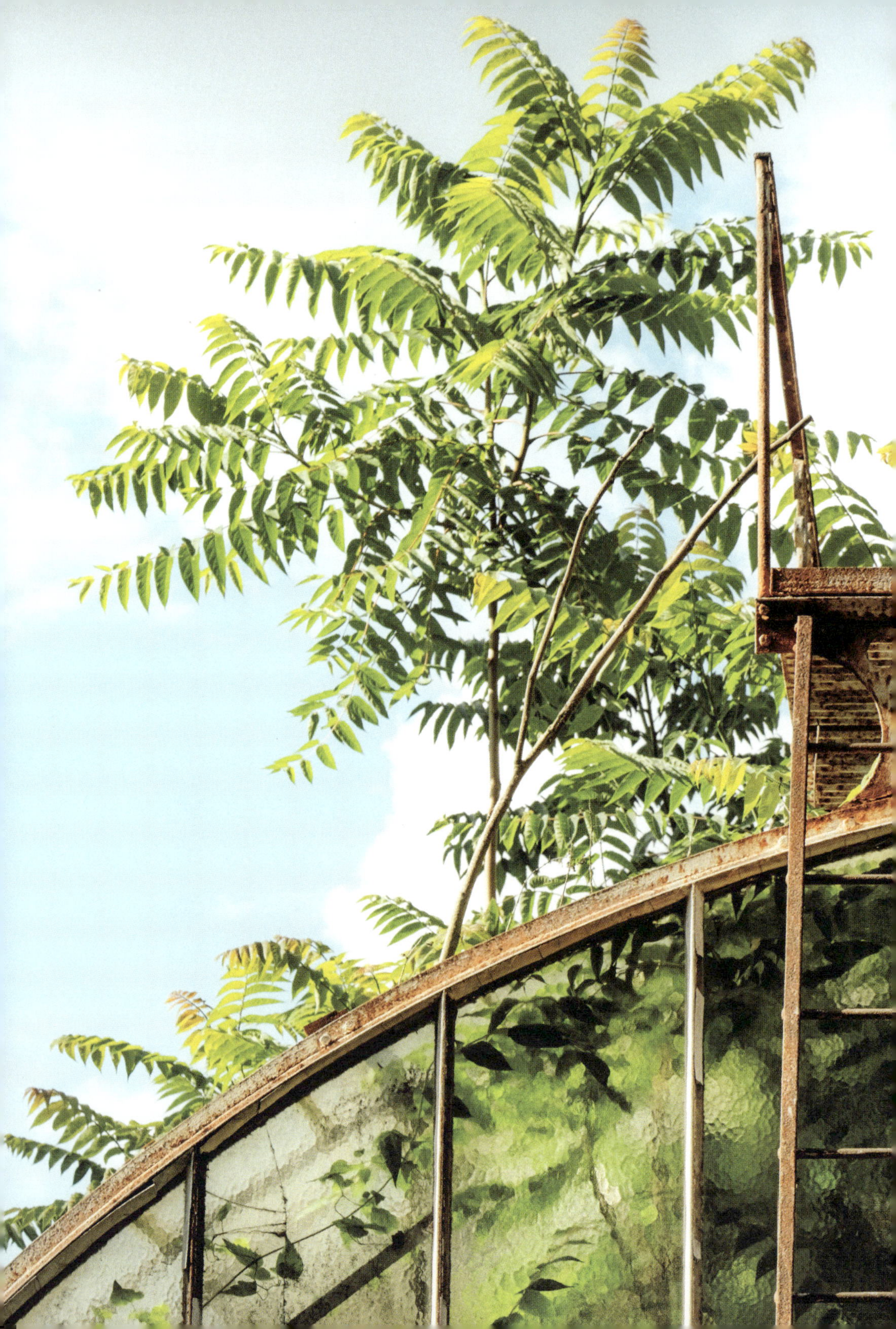

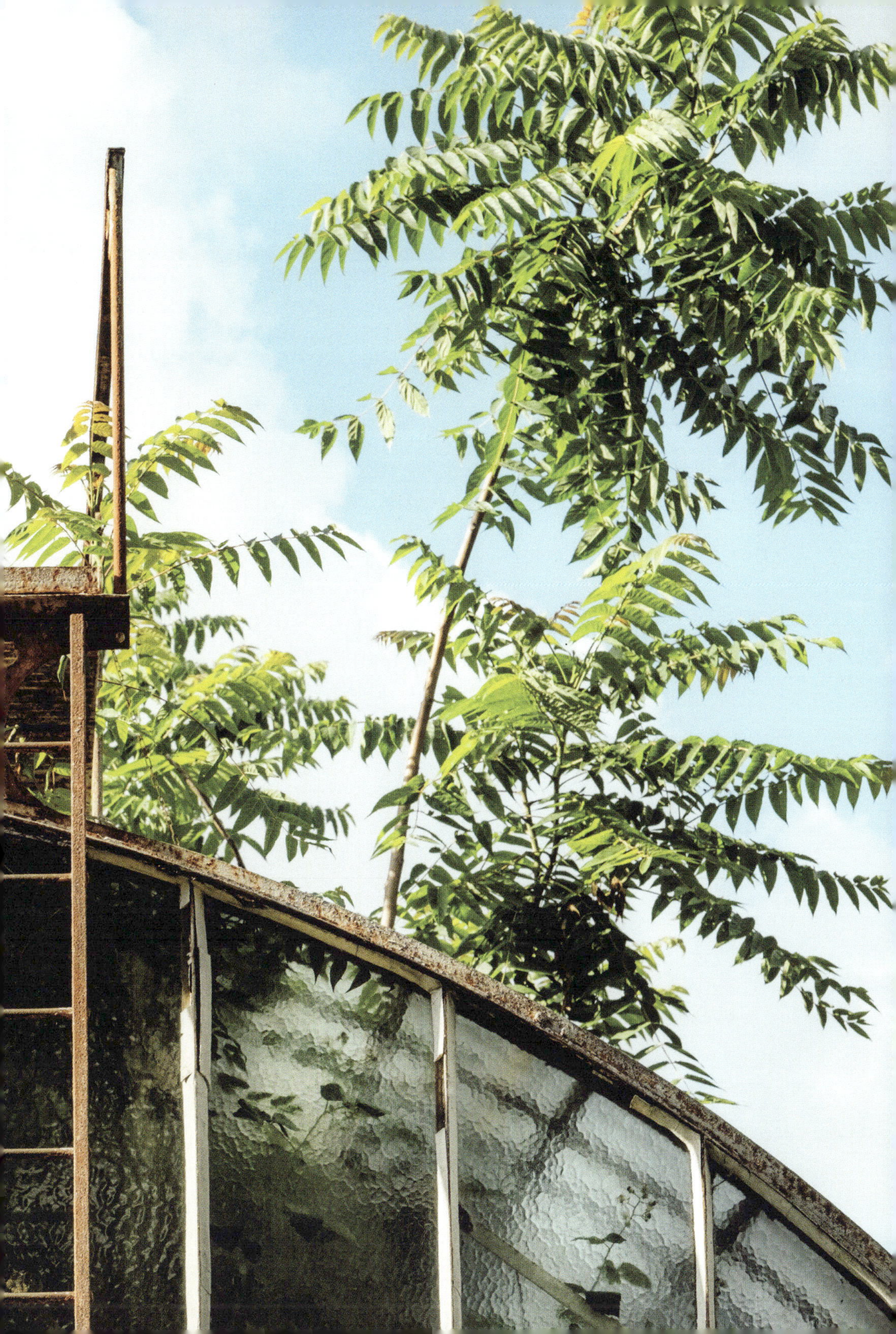

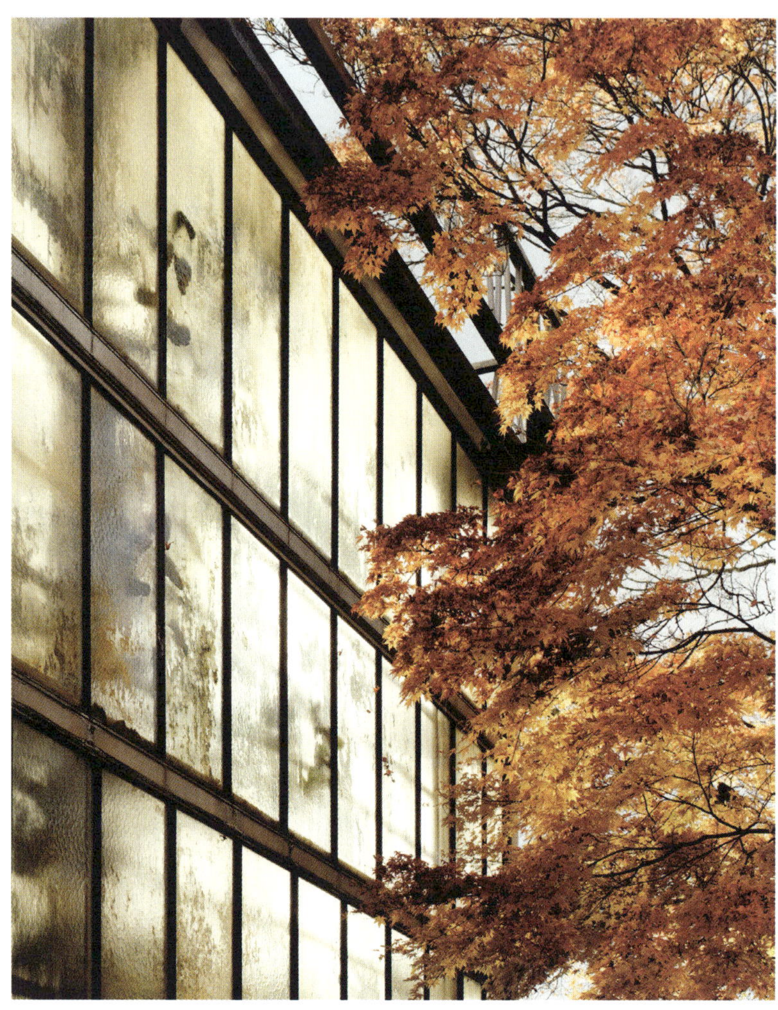

   Ghent, Belgium *(above)* Geneva, Switzerland *(opposite)*

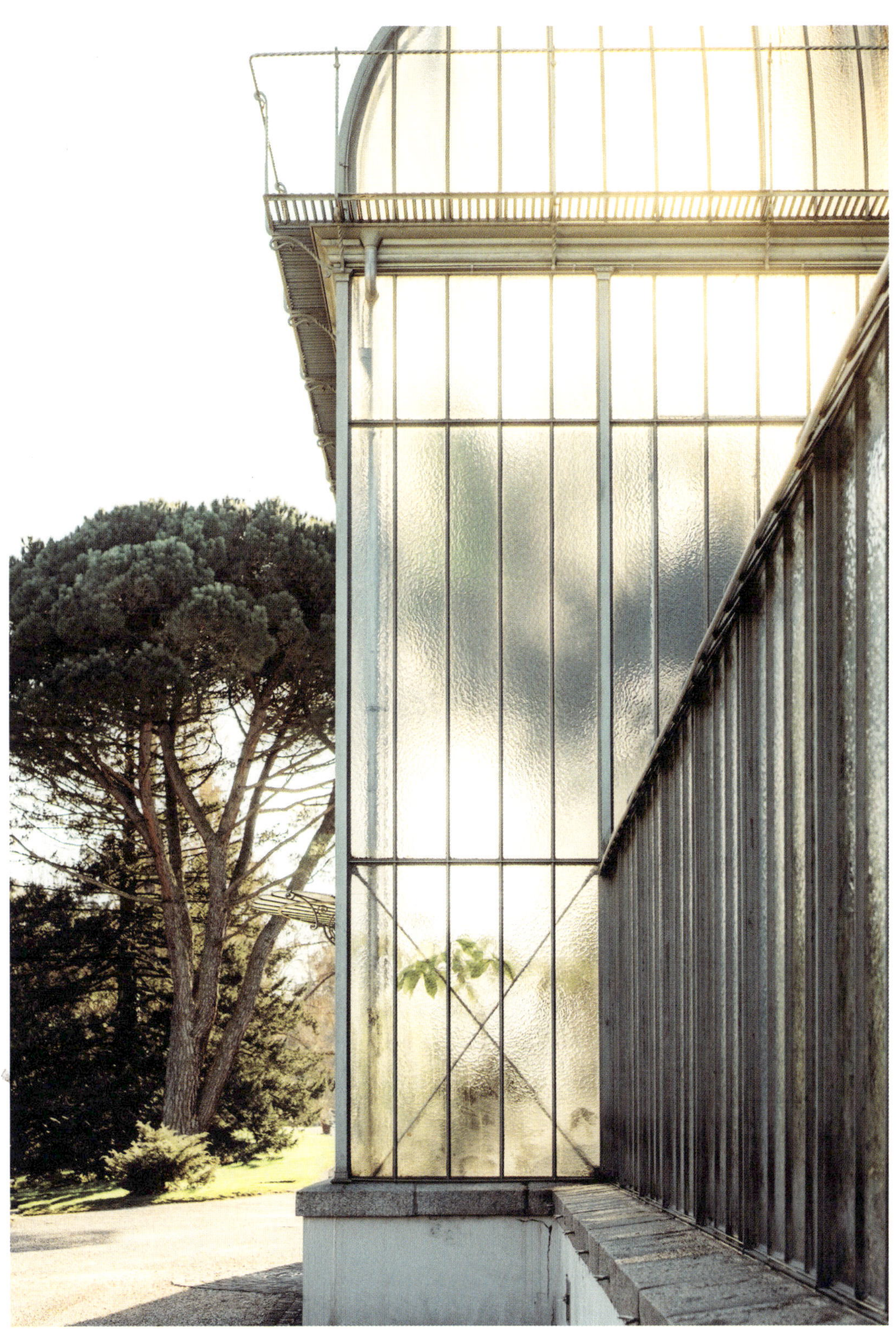

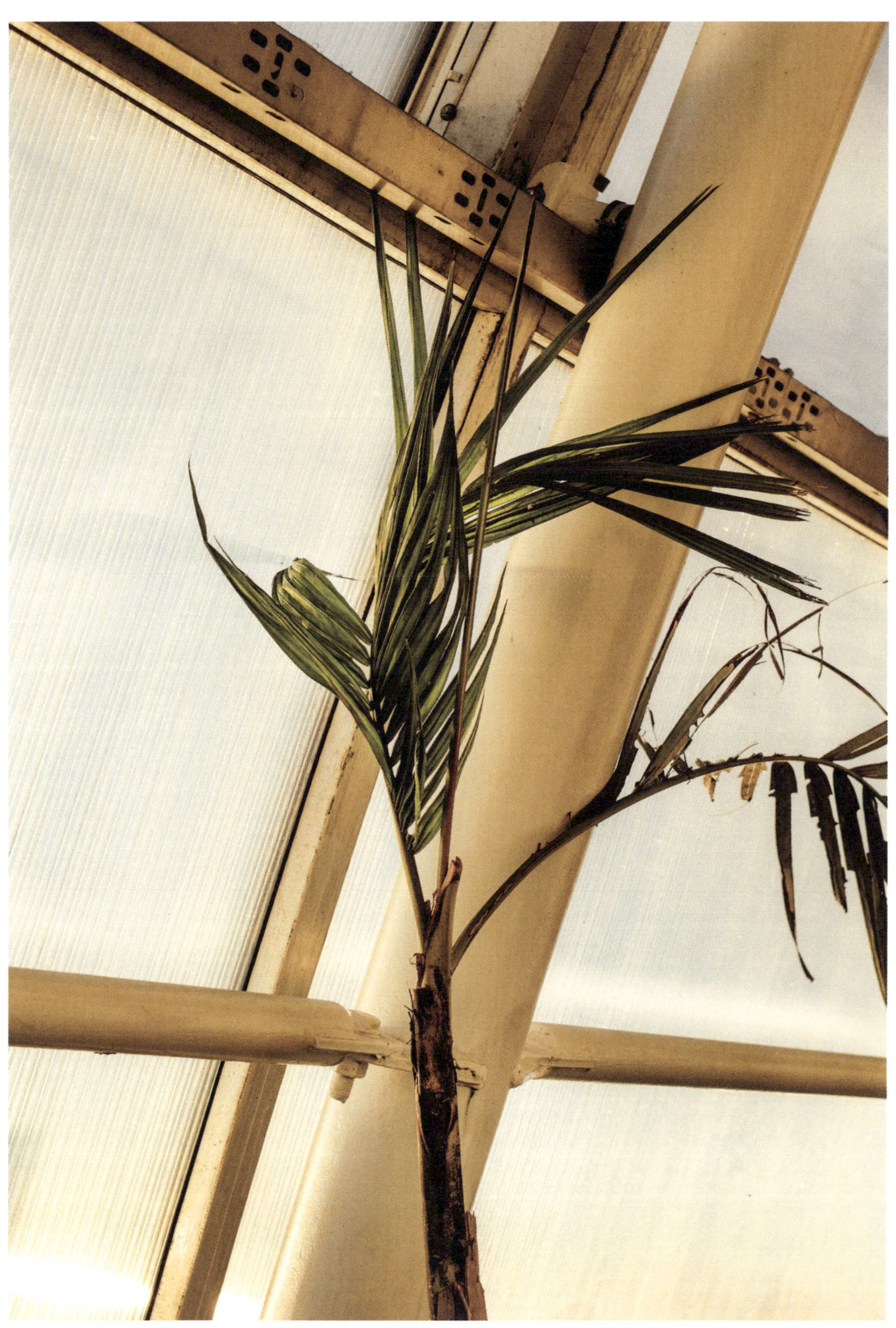

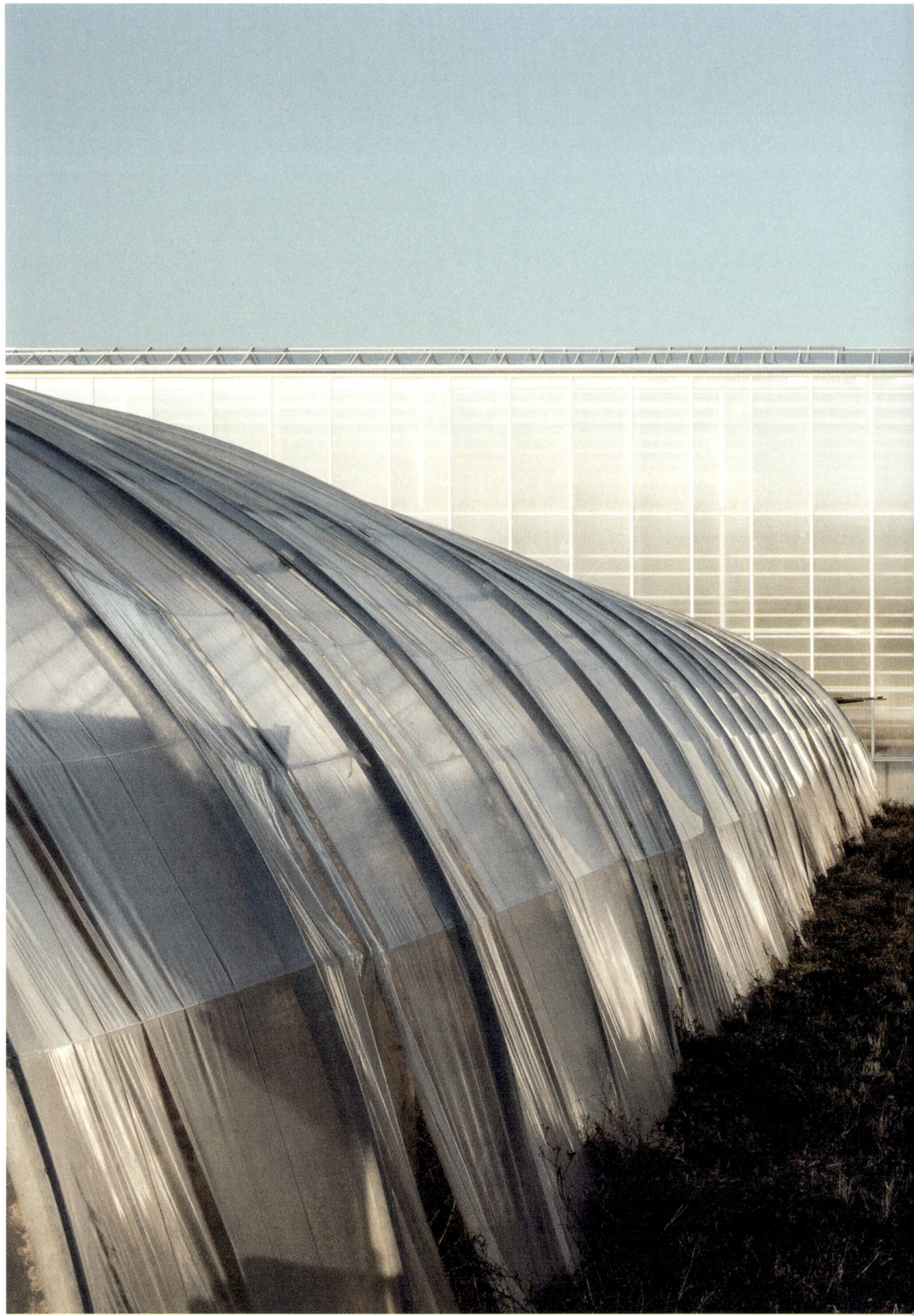

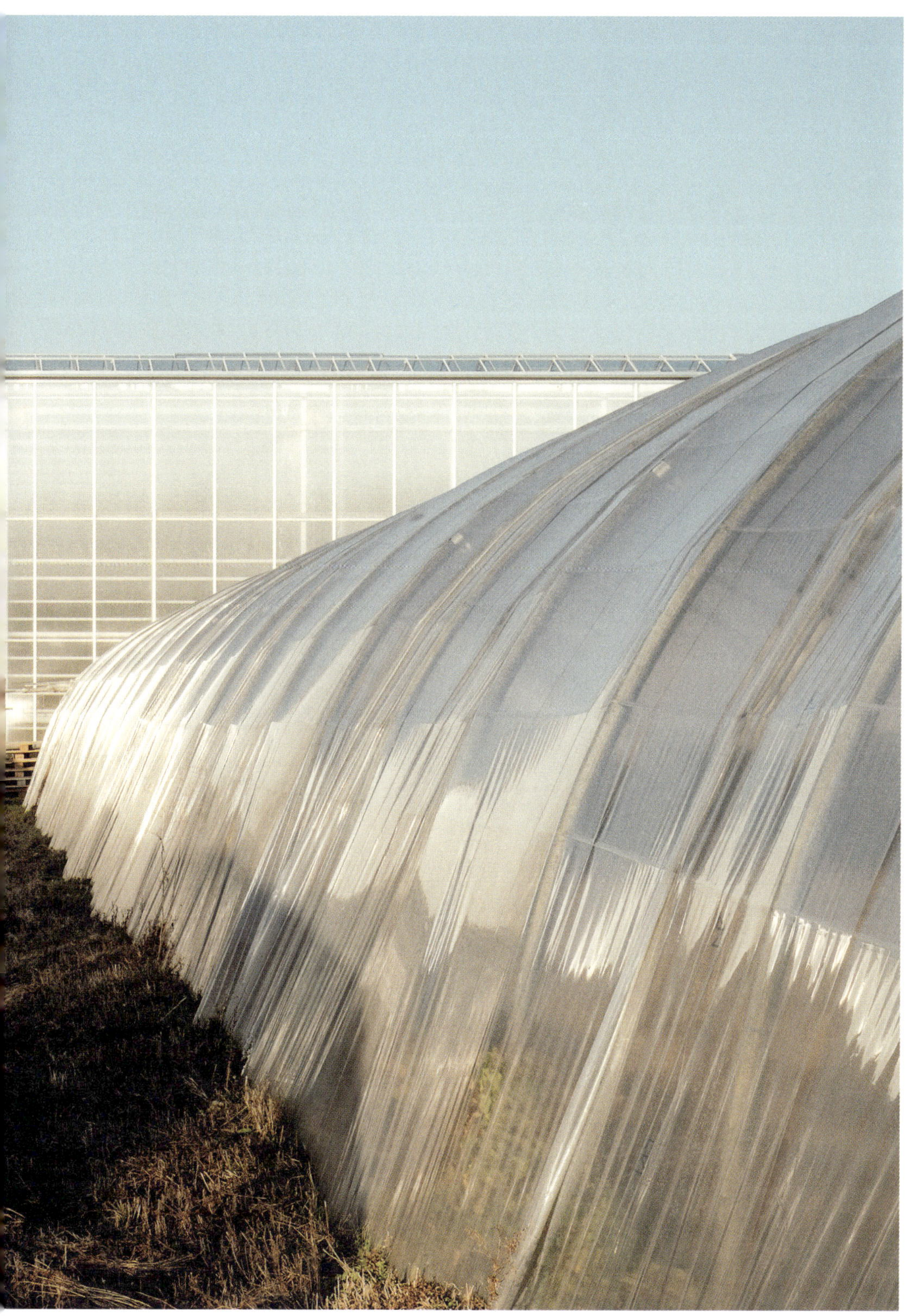

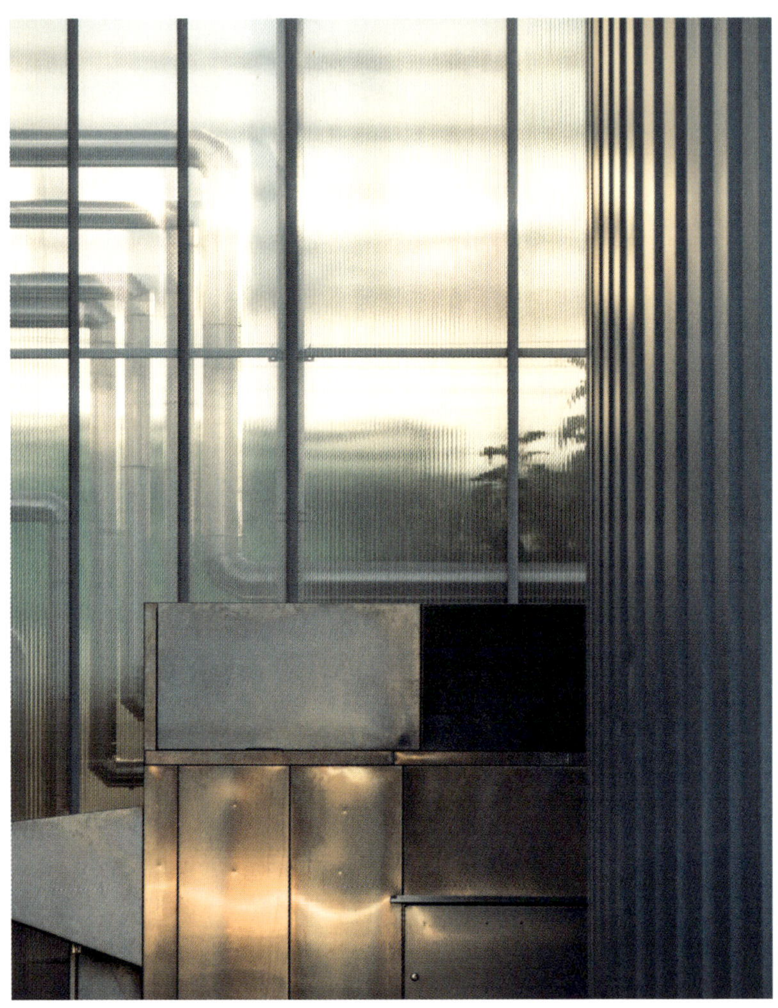

134   Near Geneva, Switzerland *(previous, above & opposite)*

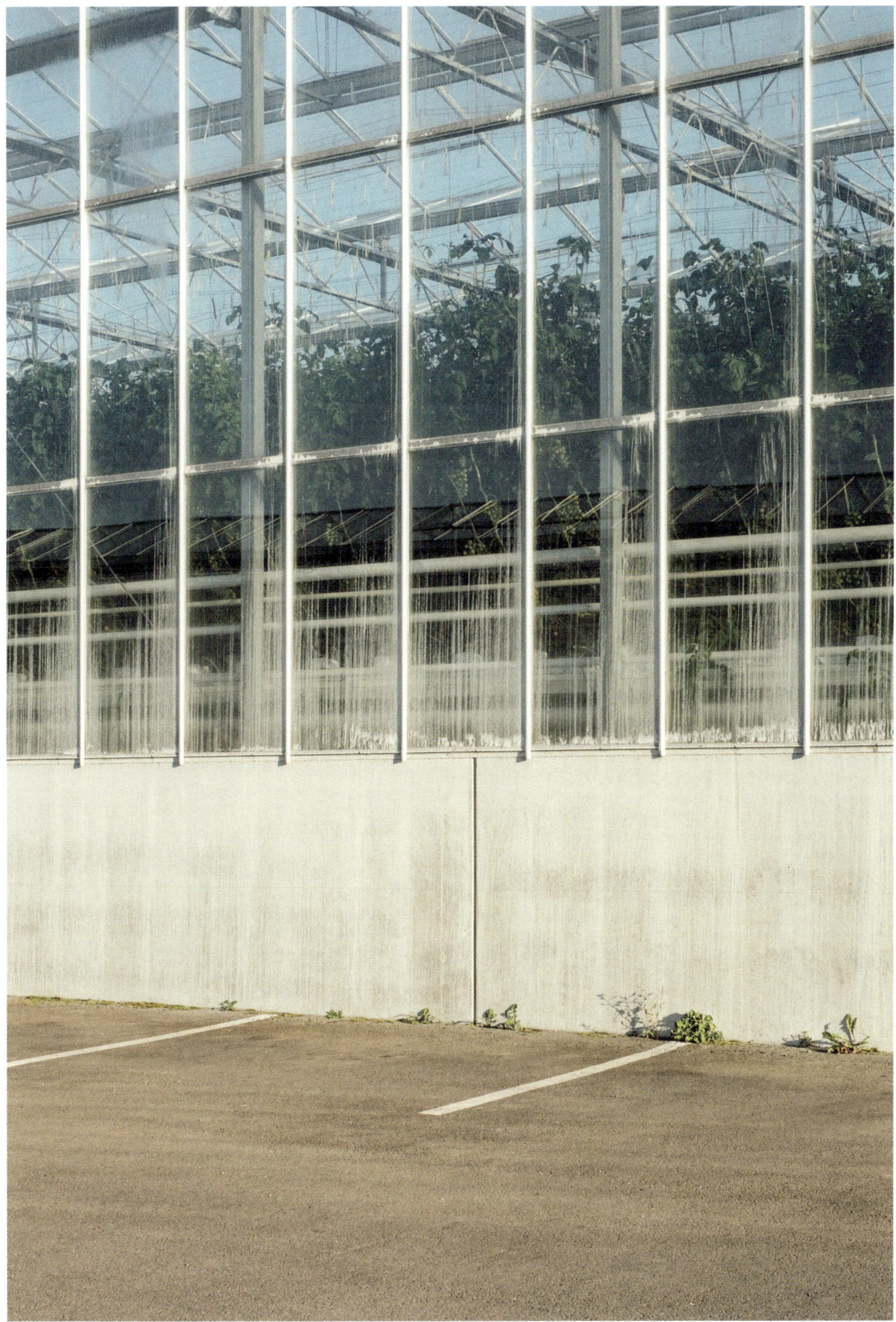

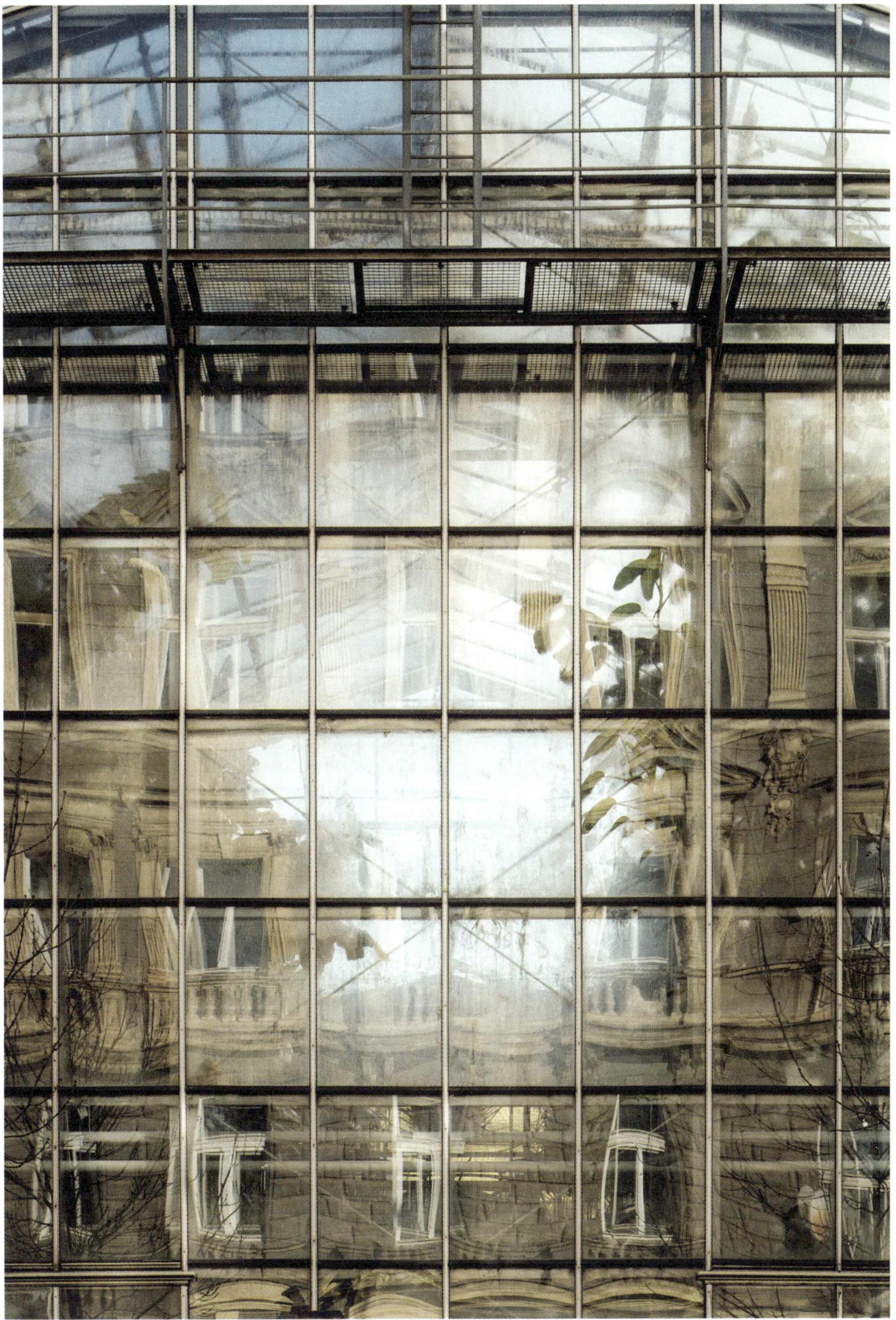

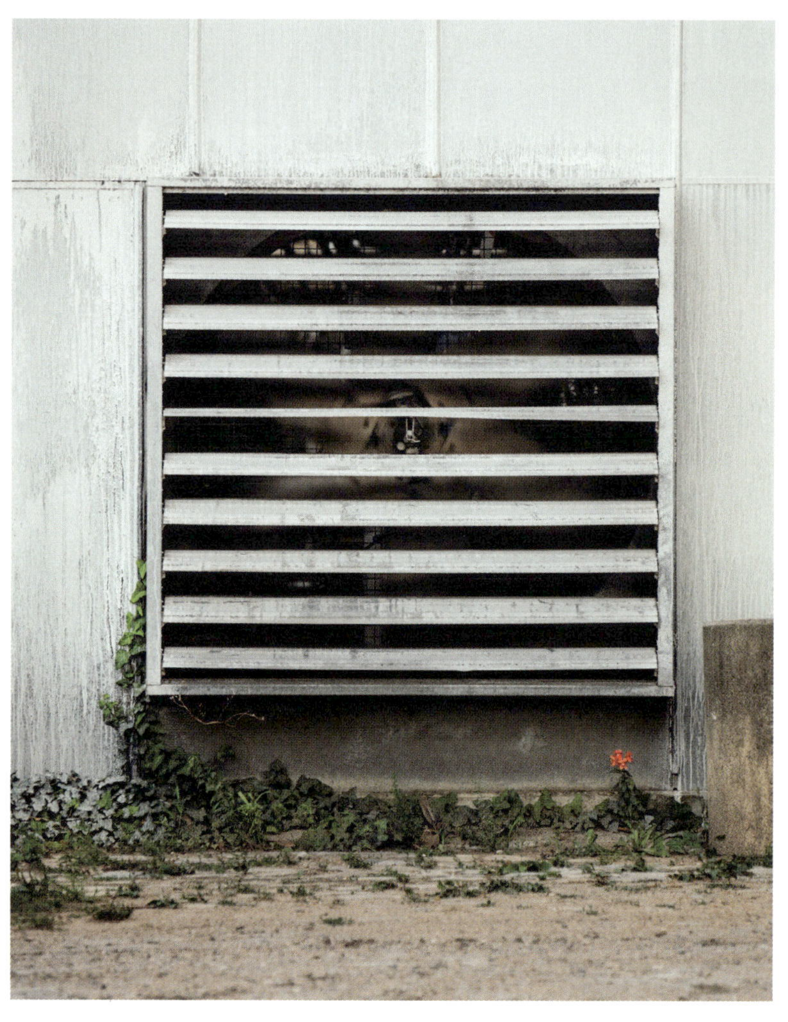

Lyon, France *(above)* Glasgow, Scotland *(opposite)*
  Near Geneva, Switzerland *(overleaf)*

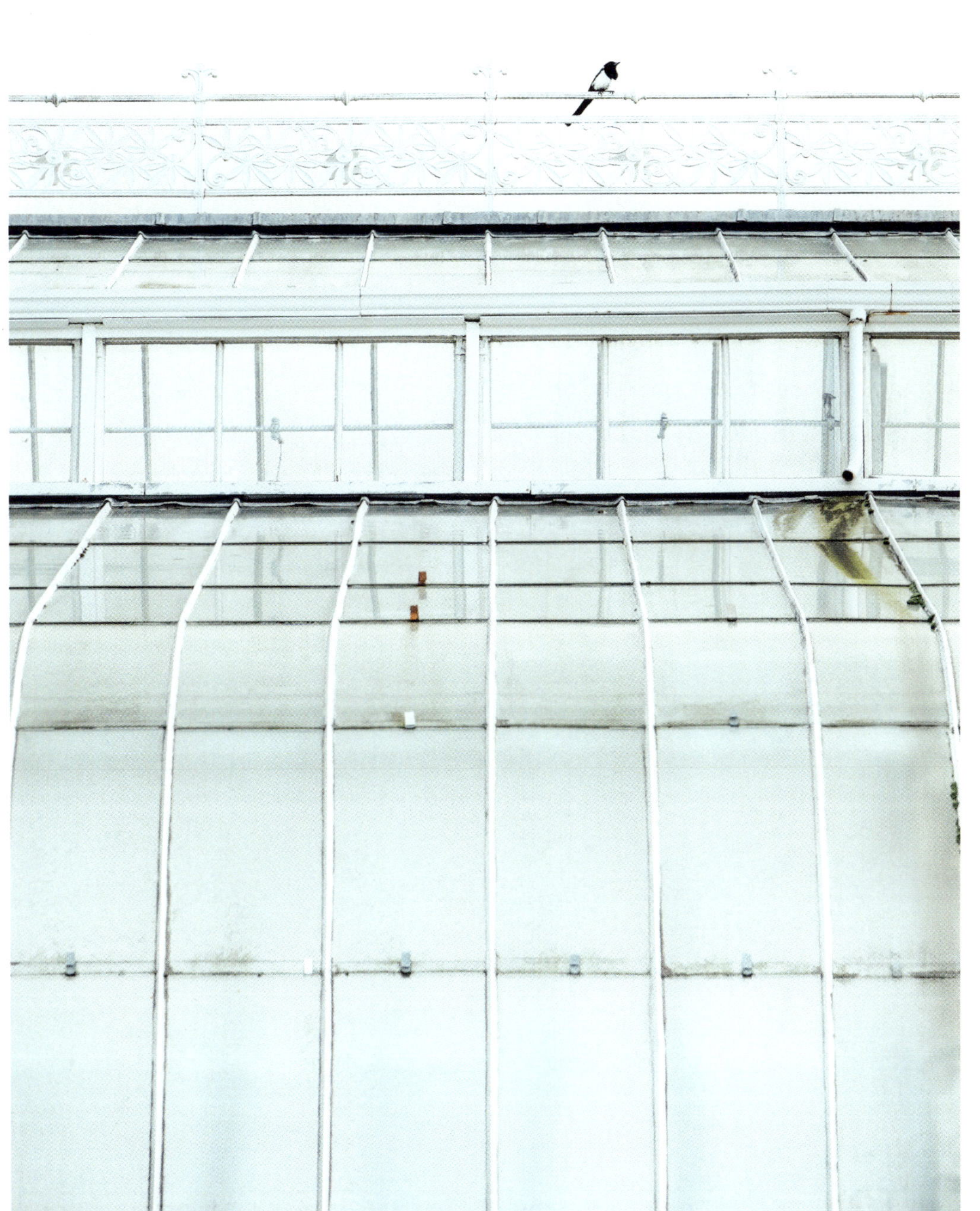

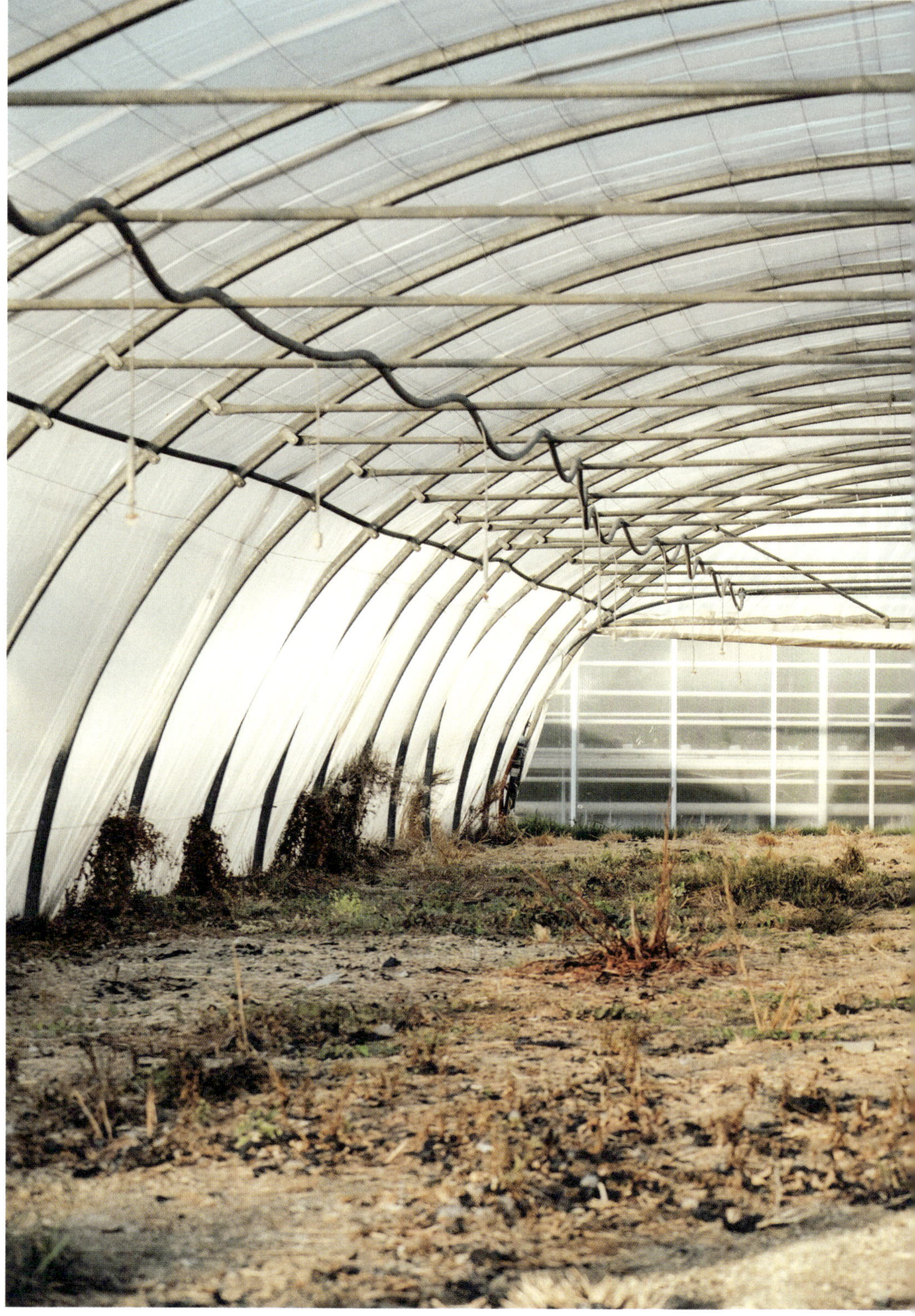

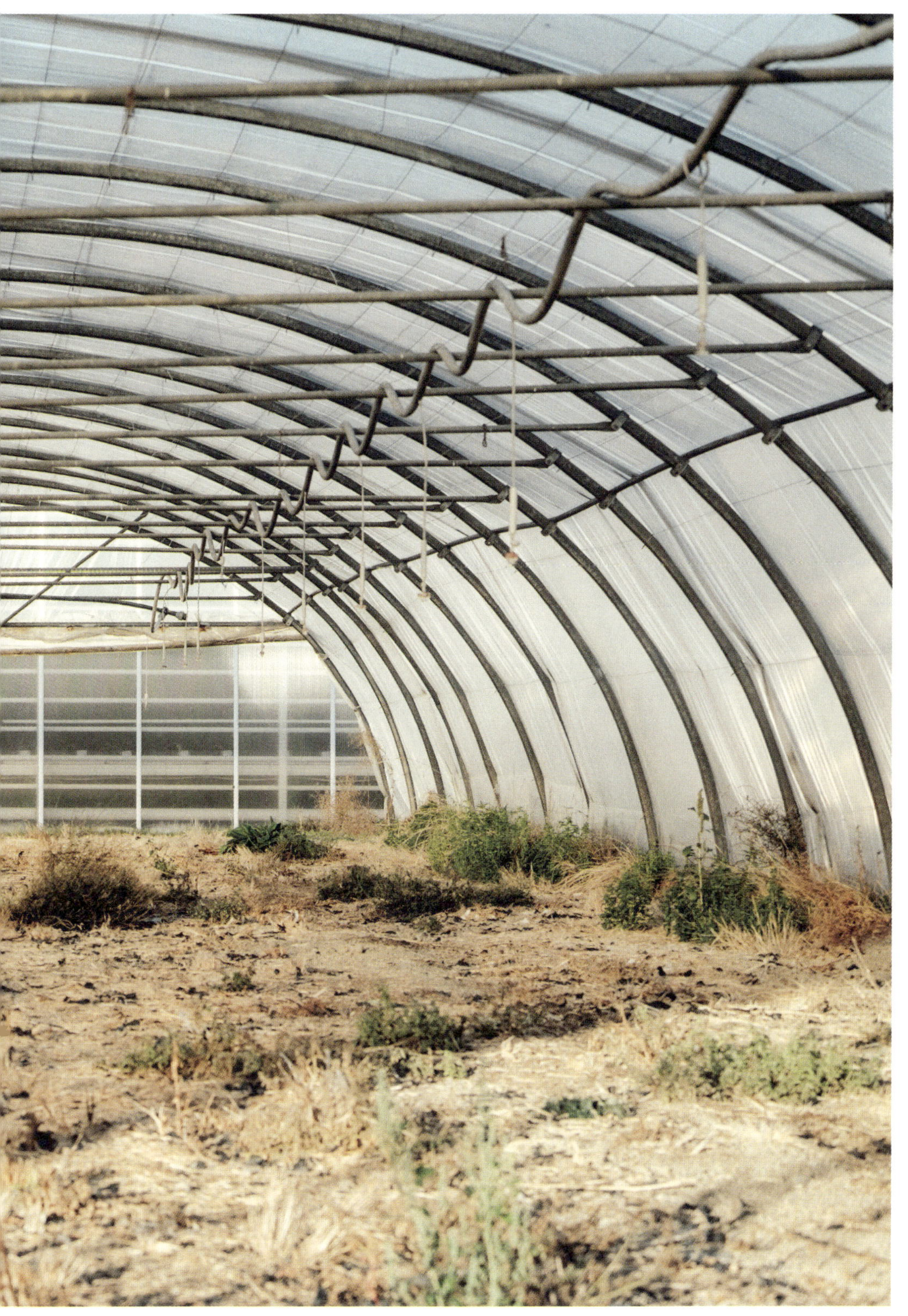

PLANT IDENTIFICATIONS

ABERDEEN
p 105 hibiscus/*Hibiscus* Malvaceae

AMSTERDAM
pp 14–15 Java fig/*Ficus benjamina*
   Moraceae
   traveller's tree/*Ravenala madagascariensis*
   Strelitziaceae
   bread tree/*Encephalartos sp.* Zamiaceae
   palm/Arecaceae
p 88 shellbark hickory/*Carya laciniosa*
   Juglantaceae

BRNO
p 48 figwort/Scrophulariaceae
p 118 date palm/*Phoenix sp.* Arecaceae

BRUSSELS
p 51 bleeding heart vine/*Clerodendrum
   speciosum* Verbenaceae

DUNDEE
p 28 hydrangea/*Hydrangea macrophylla*
   Hydrangeaceae
p 67 krantz aloe/*Aloe arborescens*
   Asphodelaceae
p 69 blue plumbago/*Plumbago auriculata*
   Plumbaginaceae
p 95 Jerusalem sage/*Phlomis fruticosa*
   Lamiaceae
p 100 palm leaf begonia/*Begonia luxuriens*
   Begoniaceae
p 103 coral plant/*Russelia equisetiformis*
   Plantaginaceae
p 119 nerium/*Nerium oleander*
   Apocynaceae

EDINBURGH
p 55 rose cactus/*Pereskia sp.* Cactaceae
p 64 bamboo/Poaceae
p 65 umbrella plant/*Shefflera sp.* Araliaceae

GENEVA
p 12 grandleaf seagrape/*Coccoloba
   pubescens* Polygonaceae
   pygmy date palm/*Phoenix roblenii*
   Arecaceae
p 19 Kentia palm/*Howea forsteriana*
   Arecaceae
   Black-eyed Susan vine/*Thunbergia alata*
   Acanthaceae
p 25 tailflower/*Anthurium sp.* Arecaceae
   Medinilla sp. Melastomataceae
   palm lily/*Cordyline Cv.* Liliaceae
p 27 Bromeliaceae
p 33 crown of thorns/*Euphorbia milii*
   Euphorbiaceae
p 39 date palm/*Phoenix sp.* Arecaceae
p 43 boat orchid/*Cymbidium Cv.*
   Orchidaceae
   tailflower/*Anthurium andraeanum*
   Araceae
   glory tree/*Clerodendrum splendens*
   Lamiaceae
p 59 palm/Arecaceae
p 61 China rose/*Hibiscus rosa-sinensis*
   Malvaceae
p 93 tree fern/*Cyathea sp.* Cyatheaceae
p 101 *Cinnamomum sp.* Lauraceae
p 129 rubber tree/*Hevea brasiliensis*
   Euphorbiaceae
   maritime pine/*Pinus pinaster* Pinaceae

Near GENEVA (countryside)
p 135 tomato plant/*Solanum lycopersicum*
   Solanaceae

*N.B. Where possible, Latin names have been
translated into common names. When only a
family name and/or genus has been identified
in Latin (i.e. Arecaceae), we have tried to
include the related common name (i.e. palm).*

Botanical

First edition, fourth printing

Copyright © Hoxton Mini Press 2020. All rights reserved.

All photographs © Samuel Zeller

Introduction by Rachel Segal Hamilton

Design and sequence by Friederike Huber and Samuel Zeller

Colour repro by Touch Digital

Latin plant identifications by Sylvester Zagato

A CIP catalogue record for this book is available from the British Library.

ISBN 978-1-910566-33-6

First published in the United Kingdom in 2018 by Hoxton Mini Press.
No part of this publication may be reproduced, stored in a retrieval system,
or transmitted in any form or by any means, electronic, mechanical,
photocopying, recording or otherwise, without the prior written
permission of the copyright owner.

Printed and bound by: Livonia Print, Latvia

To order books, collector's editions and signed prints please go to:
www.hoxtonminipress.com

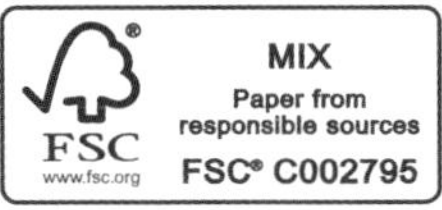